The Interface Effect

For Reed Fulton, Amos Wood, and Frances Wood, writers

The Interface Effect

ALEXANDER R. GALLOWAY

polity

The right of Alexander R. Galloway to be identified as Author of this Work has
been asserted in accordance with the UK Copyright, Designs and Patents Act 1988.

First published in 2012 by Polity Press
Reprinted in 2012, 2013 (twice)

Polity Press
65 Bridge Street
Cambridge CB2 1UR, UK

Polity Press
350 Main Street
Malden, MA 02148, USA

ISBN-13: 978-0-7456-6252-7 (hardback)
ISBN-13: 978-0-7456-6253-4 (paperback)

A catalogue record for this book is available from the British Library.

Typeset in 11 on 13 pt Scala
by Toppan Best-set Premedia Limited
Printed and bound in the United States of America by Edwards Brothers, Inc.

The publisher has used its best endeavors to ensure that the URLs for external
websites referred to in this book are correct and active at the time of going to press.
However, the publisher has no responsibility for the websites and can make no
guarantee that a site will remain live or that the content is or will remain
appropriate.

Every effort has been made to trace all copyright holders, but if any have been
inadvertently overlooked the publisher will be pleased to include any necessary
credits in any subsequent reprint or edition.

For further information on Polity, visit our website: www.politybooks.com

Contents

Preface

This book is about windows, screens, keyboards, kiosks, channels, sockets, and holes – or rather, about none of these things in particular and all of them simultaneously. For this is a book about thresholds, those mysterious zones of interaction that mediate between different realities. The goal of the book is twofold, to define the interface, but also to interpret it. Interfaces are not simply objects or boundary points. They are autonomous zones of activity. Interfaces are not things, but rather processes that effect a result of whatever kind. For this reason I will be speaking not so much about particular interface objects (screens, keyboards), but *interface effects*. And in speaking about them I will not be satisfied just to say an interface is defined in such and such a way, but to show how it exists that way for specific social and historical reasons. Interfaces themselves are effects, in that they bring about transformations in material states. But at the same time interfaces are themselves the effects of other things, and thus tell the story of the larger forces that engender them.

While addressing many different aspects of interface culture, the chapters of the book all illustrate, more or less, a specific interpretive method. The method shares a great deal with what Fredric Jameson calls *cognitive mapping*.[1] The times have changed slightly since he first broached the topic, and so too the present interests are somewhat different than his. But the central notion is the same, that *culture is history in representational form* (if Jameson will allow such a stunted paraphrase). The representational form is never a simple analog, though. It is a map, a reduction or indexical and symbolic topology. This "reduction" is a necessary trauma resulting from the impossibility of thinking the global in the here and now, of reading the present as historical. Thus the truth of social life as a whole is increasingly incompatible with its own expression. Culture emerges from this incompatibility. The same goes for the interface: it emerges from this incompatibility; it *is* this incompatibility.

Yet one might also invert the claim: socio-cultural production indeed "expresses" social life as a whole, which itself is in something of a perpetual crisis – whether that crisis be called planetary civil war, global warming and ecological collapse, increasing material fragmentation and exploitation, or simply capitalism, which after all is the engine for all the others. (Jameson admittedly follows the same broad declension narrative evident in all manner of modern-era criticism from Walter Benjamin and Theodor Adorno to Max Weber, Ferdinand Tönnies, and even of course the later Martin Heidegger.)[2] Hence specific historical traumas migrate into an excessively large number of possible representational forms.

But the cognitive map is also something more than the mirror of geopolitical crises. It is subject formation plain and simple, as the individual negotiates his or her own orientation within the world system. This means that the cognitive map is also the act of reading. It is the hermeneutic process itself, replete with all the inconsistencies and half-truths that accompany the interpretive process. So it is a trauma – in the psychoanalytic sense – as a necessary cutting that is constitutive of the self. But it is simultaneously a subject-centered induction of world experience – in the phenomenological sense. The interface effect is perched there, on the mediating thresholds of self and world.

In the pages that follow, I shall attempt to migrate Jameson's methodology slightly in the direction of new media, as any amount of historical specificity today would demand. The reader will need to determine exactly how this migration takes place, what it means, and indeed if it is successful. But the spirit of the thing is that, as will become more evident in Chapter 2 on ideology, *digital media ask a question to which the political interpretation is the only coherent answer.* In other words, digital media interpellate the political interpretation. If "digital media" is understood as our contemporary techno-culture and the "political interpretation" is understood as an attempt to read the present as material history, then indeed we are deep in Jamesonian territory.

For poetic flourish though, if nothing else, I might propose a new name for this project, *the control allegory*. Further definition of such a method, as it reveals itself in the analysis of a number of artifacts drawn from interface culture, is the project of the pages to come.

Acknowledgments

This book constitutes the final volume of *Allegories of Control*, a trio of publications on networks, games, and interfaces that examines the politics and aesthetics of information technology.

Many colleagues and friends have helped inspire and formulate the ideas, and sometimes the words, contained herein. I am grateful to all of them, and in particular to Wendy Chun, Jeff Guess, Mark Hansen, Ben Kafka, Katherine Hayles, Juliet Jacobson, David Parisi, Sarah Resnick, Jason Smith, Matthew Smith, Eugene Thacker, and McKenzie Wark. Parts of the book were originally inspired by a seminar on the interface organized by Eric de Bruyn at the University of Groningen in 2007, and then further developed on the invitation of Siegfried Zielinski for the International Flusser Lecture in Berlin in 2008. Herbert Tucker proposed a number of important improvements to Chapter 1; likewise Lisa Nakamura to the postscript. Sonaar Luthra provided valuable research assistance. I also acknowledge and thank my students, in particular those from my Fall 2010 seminar on "The Politics of Code," for allowing me to workshop material from this book.

The introduction incorporates material from "What is New Media? Ten Years After *The Language of New Media*," *Criticism* 53, no. 3 (Summer 2011): 377–384, "The Anti-Language of New Media," *Discourse* 32, no. 3 (Fall, 2010): 276–284, and "If the Cinema Is an Ontology, the Computer Is an Ethic" in *Kittler Now*, edited by Stephen Sale (Polity, forthcoming). Chapter 1 was first published in English in *New Literary History* 39, no. 4 (Autumn 2009): 931–955 and in German in the International Flusser Lecture pamphlet series as *Außer Betrieb: Das müßige Interface* (Cologne: Walther König, 2010). Chapter 2 was first published as "Language Wants To Be Overlooked: On Software and Ideology," *Journal of Visual Culture* 5, no. 3 (December 2006): 315–331. Chapter 3 was first published in *Theory, Culture & Society* 28, nos. 7–8 (December 2011): 85–102. Chapter 4 was first published as "24/7, 16.8: Is 24 a Political Show?," *Afterimage: The Journal of Media Arts and Cultural Criticism* 35, no. 1 (July–August, 2007): 18–22 (see www.vsw. org/ai). The postscript was first published as "Does the Whatever Speak?" in *Race After the Internet*, edited by Lisa Nakamura and Peter Chow-White (New York: Routledge, 2011). I thank these journals and presses for allowing this material, now altered and updated, to reappear here in a new form.

Introduction: The Computer as a Mode of Mediation

What Are New Media?

First a frank assessment: There are very few books on new media worth reading. Just when the nay-sayers decry the end of the written word, bookstore shelves still overflow with fluff on digital this and digital that. And even as a countervailing chorus emerged that was more skeptical of the widespread adoption of new media – in France Jacques Chirac once spoke disparagingly about "that Anglo-Saxon network" (for, as anyone knows, in the beginning there was Minitel) – it was evident that the Internet revolution had already taken place in the US, in Europe, and elsewhere. Like it or not the new culture is networked and open source, and one is in need of intelligent interventions to evaluate it. In the years since its original publication in 2001, Lev Manovich's *The Language of New Media* has become one of the most read and cited texts on the topic.[1] It is a key entry in the disciplines of poetics and cultural aesthetics, and has helped define the new field of software studies. So I will start with Manovich, deferring to the influence of the text, and betting that it might already be familiar to readers. The book is not without its limitations, however, and perhaps today we may begin to look again on the text with the fresh eyes of historical distance, and, using the book as a springboard into other topics, reassess many different aspects of cultural and aesthetic life, from our tools to our texts, from our bodies to our social relations, from our digital objects to our digital interfaces.

Internet culture spawned *The Language of New Media*, particularly the first generation of 1990s web culture. What this means is that the book is the product of a specific sliver of history when the conditions of the production and distribution of knowledge were rather different than they are today. What was once a subversive medium is now a spectacle playground like any other. The first phase of web culture, one must admit, carried a revolutionary impulse; call it the Saint-Just to today's imperial era. Manovich's book is a product of that first phase. Walls were coming down, hierarchies were crumbling, the old brick and mortar society was giving way to a new digital universe. On the one hand, new virulent ways of looking at the world were forming with unprecedented ferocity – sometimes conveniently labeled the "California ideology" – coalescing around the neoliberal impulse to open source everything (information wants to be free, desire wants to be free, capital wants to be free) and the promise to liberate mankind in ways only dreamed of by our forebears in the new social movements of the 1960s. On the other hand, amid this process of leveling, a new Republic of Letters began to form using email and bulletin-board systems that seemed to offer a real intellectual and social community devoted to the exploration and critique of new media. *The Language of New Media* is a product of this community. Discussed and refined in online forums like Nettime, and partially previewed prior to publication on the email list Rhizome (a web site named enthusiastically, if naively, after the emancipatory topology described in Deleuze and Guattari), *The Language of New Media* was written for, within, and against the new Internet culture of the late 1990s.

Looking back like this is not to suggest that we should dwell on previous decades with nostalgic yearning for a simpler time, nor that Manovich's book has nothing more to say to us today. On the contrary, the simple premise of the book – that new media may be defined via reference to a foundational language or set of formal and poetic qualities identified across all sorts of new media objects, and indeed across historical and social context – suggests the opposite approach: we are *required* to think critically and historically because of the very fact that the digital is so structural, so abstract, so synchronic.

Manovich's strength lies in the description of digital technologies as poetic and aesthetic objects. His book aims to be a kind of general textbook on new media. Manovich begins from his own experience with software, then he extends his observations so that the "telling detail" becomes a piece in a larger system.

Is Manovich's view on the world a modernist one? I think so. His is a modernist lens in the sense that he returns again and again to the formal essence of the medium, the techniques and characteristics of the technology, and then uses these qualities to talk about the new (even if he ends up revealing that it is not as new as we thought it was). This is illustrated most vividly in the conceptual heart of the book, part one entitled "What Is New Media?" Here Manovich offers a number of defining principles for digital technology, and at the same time debunks several of the myths surrounding it. The five principles – numeric representation, modularity, automation, variability, and transcoding – are not to be understood as universal laws of new media. Rather, they describe some of the aesthetic properties of data, and the basic ways in which information is created, stored, and rendered intelligible.

Scattered throughout the book, Manovich advances a number of aesthetic claims that have become commonplace parlance in the discourse on digital interfaces, including the idea of a "logic of selection," the importance of compositing, the way in which the database itself is a medium, the emphasis on navigation through space, the reversal of the relationship between syntagm and paradigm, the centrality of games and play, the waning of temporal montage (and the rise of spatial montage), and many other observations. All of these concepts and claims are now taken for granted in the various debates that make up today's discourse on new media.

Dissent exists of course. Given that the operative question is "What Is New Media?" we should remember that more than one response exists to such a question.[2] It is clear where Manovich puts his favor: new media are essentially *software applications*. But others have answered the same question in very different ways. There are those who say that hardware is as important if not more so than software (Friedrich Kittler or

Wendy Hui Kyong Chun), or those who focus on the new forms of social interaction that media do or do not facilitate (Geert Lovink or Yochai Benkler), or even those who focus on networks of information rather than simply personal computers (Tiziana Terranova or Eugene Thacker). Perhaps because of the wide degree of latitude afforded by the topic, Manovich's book has elicited a healthy stream of dialogue and debate since its original publication. I for one consider his claim about "the myth of interactivity" (55) to be misguided: yes, the term "interactive" is practically meaningless due to overuse, but that does not mean the term should apply willy-nilly to static works of art. But such quibbles are neither here nor there.

Rather, I would like to spotlight two issues of more profound significance that are worth addressing in the book. The first has to do with *cinema*, the second with *history*.

As the opening pages divulge, the dirty little secret of *The Language of New Media*, and the detail that reveals Manovich's first passion, is this: cinema was the first new media. New media did not begin in the 1980s in Silicon Valley; it began a hundred years prior at Étienne-Jules Marey's Station Physiologique in the outskirts of Paris. The reason for this is that cinema is the first medium to bring together techniques like compositing, recombination, digital sampling (the discrete capture of photographic images at a fixed rate through time), and machine automation, techniques that, of course, are present in other media, but never as effectively as the singular synthesis offered by the cinema. Thus, the technique of layering inside Photoshop is simply the same technique used in the color key effects afforded by video, or the cinematic convention of shooting actors standing in front of a rear-screen projection backdrop. Or to choose another example, the binary zero-and-one samples of a digital music file are also present decades earlier in the on and off regularity of a single film frame transiting across the projector's beam, stopping for a split second, and then moving again. For Manovich the flicker of film was always already a digital flicker.

With such fuel for controversy, many were quick to confront Manovich on his claims, perhaps most notably Mark B. N. Hansen in his book *New Philosophy for New Media*. Hansen acknowledges the influence of *The Language of New Media*, writing that "Manovich's depiction of digital technology is undoubtedly the most rich and detailed available today."[3] Yet he also argues that Manovich's book is tinted by an over investment in the cinematic. Manovich's position "extends the sway of the 'cinematic' in the narrow sense, and in particular serves to ratify cinematic immobility *as the default condition of the human-computer interface*."[4] (Yet Hansen's subsequent claim, that Manovich cannot think beyond the rectilinear cinematic frame, is unconvincing, given Manovich's argument in the book about the waning of temporal montage and the rise of spatial montage, or what is often simply called "windowing.") In short, Manovich's greatest trick, the cinema, is also, in the eyes of some critics, his greatest vulnerability.

In addition to cinema, a second large issue looms in the book, that of history. Would it be entirely correct to say that this book has no interest in the social, that it has no interest in the political, that it is blinded (by poetics and formal structure) from seeing history itself? As with anyone who gravitates to pure poetics, Manovich is not immune to such questions. Like some of his critics, I too am concerned by the emphasis on poetics and pure formalism. One might think of Manovich as the polar opposite of someone like Fredric Jameson and the commitment to what he calls the "poetics of social forms." One sees the poetics in Manovich, but one loses the social forms. So there is something to be said for the argument that Manovich is participating in the tradition of those media theorists, like Kittler or Marshall McLuhan, who, while they may discuss the embeddedness of media systems within social or historical processes, ultimately put a premium on media as pure formal devices. (Kittler's politics are complicated, but in general he falls prey to some of the same traps of nostalgia and Hellenistic longing as his romantic forebears; McLuhan knew which way the wind was blowing in his public persona, but in private was a good traditional catholic who was more than a little unnerved by the social upheavals happening around him.)

Near to his heart, Manovich opens the book with Dziga Vertov. Featuring the Soviet filmmaker so prominently did not

go unnoticed by the intellectual establishment. In the following passage he is held at arm's length by the editors of the
journal *October*, a publication known to have a special relationship to the avant-garde as well as poststructuralism and continental philosophy:

> It is thus with some interest that we witness the usage of a crucial
> avant-garde film such as Dziga Vertov's *Man with a Movie Camera*
> as the opening device of a recent text on the "language of new
> media," just as it once provided the signal image some years ago
> for the very first issue of this journal. And it is also with some
> doubt that we listen to these same theoreticians of the new digital
> media proclaim that cinema and photography – with their indexi-
> cal, archival properties – were merely preliminary steps on the
> path to their merging with the computer in the *über*-archive of the
> database. Much of what was most important to cinema and pho-
> tography is wiped away by such a teleology. And much of what
> seems most critical in contemporary artistic practice reacts to just
> such an erasure.[5]

Going a step further, Brian Holmes continues this line of
dissent, as he bemoans what he sees as Manovich's "smug
insistence that the new media were essentially defined by a
certain kind of rhythm, a certain multiplication of screens, a
certain connection to databases, etc. – in other words, that the
new media were essentially defined by the dominant trends of
contemporary capitalist society."[6]

While such dismissals might be seductive, here too I am
not entirely convinced, and perhaps against my better judg-
ment wish to offer something of a defense on his behalf. Yes,
Manovich refuses a specific kind of American or European
politico-historical critique of media technologies, the kind we
might associate with any number of theorists on the left, from
Louis Althusser, to Jean Baudrillard, to Guy Debord, or even
today with Giorgio Agamben or Bernard Stiegler. But to understand Manovich, one must understand two important aspects
of his work.

In an important short essay from 1996, "On Totalitarian
Interactivity," Manovich admits that he sees digital interactivity as a type of political manipulation. He harbors a deep-

seated phobia of political ideology, due largely to his youth spent in the Soviet Union:

> As a post-communist subject, I cannot but see [the] Internet as a communal apartment of [the] Stalin era: no privacy, everybody spies on everybody else, [an] always present line for common areas such as the toilet or the kitchen. Or I can think of it as a giant garbage site for the information society, with everybody dumping their used products of intellectual labor and nobody cleaning up. Or as a new, Mass Panopticon (which was already realized in communist societies) – complete transparency, everybody can track everybody else.[7]

These kinds of passages should put to rest any murmurs over whether or not Manovich has a knowledge of history. By the early 1930s, Stalin had made socialist realism the only possible style in the Soviet Union. During this period the Russian formalists were criticized for not paying enough attention to social and historical issues, in essence for being apolitical. The power of the Stalinist machine eventually forced many of these formalists to the margins, or worse, into exile or death. Of course Manovich is no exiled enemy of the state, but because of this history he considers it intellectually dangerous to deny questions of form, poetics, and aesthetics. The irony is that, in making this gesture, which Manovich would classify as a gesture of political independence in the face of state power, he has been accused of overlooking the political sphere entirely. What worked one way in the Eastern Bloc, apparently works another way in the contemporary West.

His apparent abdication of the political (and his taking up the question of poetics), then, must not be measured against an Americo-European leftist yardstick, but as a kind of *glasnost* of the digital. Manovich is saying, in essence: the technological infrastructure may or may not have dubious politics, but let us put the old hobbyhorse of the critique of state-driven ideology behind us and dive into the semiotics of software so that we may first understand how it works.

Let me acknowledge therefore – and this is the second aspect – that Manovich's political gesture exists, even if it is a

counter-intuitive one. He is not a politicized Western intellectual in the Sartrean mold. But that is the point. In other
words, when he writes on Vertov, he slices Vertov free from
the grasp of traditions such as "The Dziga Vertov Group" and
other red-flag comrades wishing a neat and tidy equation
between radical aesthetic experiments and radical politics. In
Manovich a medium is never a *dispositif*. (Mind you, I am not
endorsing this myself, merely attempting to offer a charitable
description of it.) Manovich would rather make the argument
that new media are first and foremost aesthetic objects. His
proof for this is, ironically, a profoundly historical one, that
Vertov simply does not have the same status today as he did
during the early and middle twentieth century. In an age when
Vertov's cinematic principles are embodied in code and
bundled as mere filter effects for desktop movie-making software, as they are today, the revolutionary power of radical
aesthetics seems rather deflated. When Jean-Luc Godard
becomes a plug-in, we must look beyond the Nouvelle Vague.
Manovich understands this. His book thus serves as a provocation to those who still think that formalism is politically progressive. It is not, for new media at least, and that is the point.

In the end *The Language of New Media* seems to be doing
two things at once. On the one hand it tries to outline the
specificity of new media, the particular qualities of the medium
that should be understood as absolutely new. But on the other
hand Manovich insists that new media are essentially cinematic, suggesting that we must look not to the new, but backward to the various media that have come before. "To
summarize," he writes in the middle of the book, "*the visual
culture of a computer age is cinematographic in its appearance,
digital on the level of its material, and computational (i.e., software
driven) in its logic*" (180). The use of a layer metaphor is telling.
At one layer is cinema, at a second layer are bits and bytes, at
a third algorithm. Manovich's new media thus follow the same
structure of the *mise en abîme*: an outside that leads to an
inside, which leads to another inside, and on and on. This too
shows how Manovich's methodology is implicitly historical,
for the media landscape changed fundamentally after the
invention of cybernetics in the late 1940s. Today all media are

a question of synecdoche (scaling a part for the whole), not indexicality (pointing from here to there).[8] This assumption is absolutely central in *The Language of New Media*, and it helps explain why Manovich is prompted to look *within*, to cinema, in order to look to the present.

Google or Facebook have already broached the question of the interface. The open-source culture of new media really means one thing today, it means open interfaces. It means the freedom to connect to technical images. Even source code is a kind of interface, an interface into a lower level set of libraries and operation codes. Thus, when Google or Facebook "open-sources" resource *x*, it provides an API or "Application Programming Interface" granting managed access to *x*. Let us not be fooled: open source does not mean the unvarnished truth, but rather a specific communicative artifice like any other. And in this sense one should never celebrate a piece of source code, open or closed, as a bona fide original text (whatever that might mean). The interesting question is not so much whether open source is "more open" or "less open" than other systems of knowledge, but rather the question "How does open source shape systems of storage and transmission of knowledge?" If one is willing to assent to a synecdoche model for media systems, then it follows that sources (or partial sources) will play a more important role, since the system/subsystem or whole/part arrangement necessitates that one think about the innards of things as one scales from outside to inside.

However, the bad news, or good depending on one's proclivities, is that this "source" has almost nothing to do with concerns around sources and essences from a generation or two ago, particularly the concerns native to that intellectual movement so thoroughly *gauche* today, poststructuralism. The general open sourcing of all media systems, including the human form as the most emblematic media system, has almost nothing to do with the lingering phenomenological anxiety around presence and truth fueling poststructuralism's long obsession over sources. What was once an intellectual intervention is now part of the mechanical infrastructure. And so goes the dialectical machine, co-opting critique as fuel for the new spirit of capitalism.[9] Instead one sees that the open sourcing of media systems (information wants to be free, desire wants to be free, capital wants to be free) is really about the migration into a new way of structuring information and material resources, which as Rancière might say also has its corresponding regime of art. But as in previous times one is still free to read the truth of social life through such structures – as Jameson does with his perennially useful methodology known as "cognitive mapping" – provided of course that one is not dazzled by the short-term candy of openness as such.

The dual move in Manovich – both to the past and to the present – is in fact a single gesture, for the grand argument given in his work is really one about media in general, that to mediate is really to interface, that mediation in general is just repetition in particular, and thus that the "new" media are really all the artifacts and traces of the past coming to appear in an ever expanding present.

If the Cinema Is an Ontology, the Computer Is an Ethic

T. J. Clark observed once, with the calm voice of experience, that in Courbet the entire world is one of proximity; the paintable is that thing, that space, that can be transformed into a Second Empire drawing room. This is Stanley Cavell's assessment too when, in *The World Viewed*, following Michael Fried's 1967 essay "Art and Objecthood," he likens painting to a certain desire for presentness. Painting assembles a space. But it is always a proximal space, a bounded space of textures and things brought around, not too close exactly, but certainly unconcealed and arrayed for handling. Painting is not Cavell's primary concern in *The World Viewed*, it is cinema after all, but painting offers a road down which one might travel to ascertain a certain quality shared by painting, photography, film, and a number of other art forms. It is the desire that the world be brought near to us.

Having a desire to be brought near – such a desire is most certainly at the very base of human life. Indeed the relative nearness and farness of things may account for all manner of action, from love to hate, from the joy of communion to the perils of exile. But that is not all, for in art it concerns a specific, not a general, iteration of this desire for nearness. The phenomenon is most acute in photography, and thereby, for Cavell, in cinema (for him, a photography derivative); as he puts it: the world of the image is present to us, but we were never present to it. So it is nearness with a catch. The viewer does not attend the filming of the "profilmic event," to use the parlance of cinema studies. Thus it is a desire to be brought near, but one already afflicted with a specific neurosis, that of the rejection of the self. With each attempt to array the world in proximal relation to us, we must at the same time make ourselves disappear. With each step forward in Cavell's world, one becomes that much more inert. Every step done is a step undone.

Evoking questions of ethics and responsibility, Plato writes of a magical ring, the Ring of Gyges, that grants invisibility to the wearer and thus potential immunity from moral consequence. In effect, the cinema forces us to don the Ring of Gyges, making the self an invisible half-participant in the world.[10] The self becomes a viewing self, and the world becomes a world viewed. This is, in a nutshell, the cinematic condition for Cavell, and I guess I agree with him. The penalties and rewards are clear: to be "cinematically" present to the world, to experience the pleasure of the movies, one must be a masochist. That is to say, to be in a relation of presence with the world cinematically, one must subject the self to the ultimate in pain and humiliation, which is nothing short of complete erasure. It has been said that the cinema is the most phenomenological of media. But whether this is a phenomenology or the absolute impossibility of one is not entirely clear.

Cavell wrote: "A painting *is* a world; a photograph is *of* a world."[11] What can one say then of the cinema? Or the computer? Paraphrasing Cavell's definition of cinema, one might say, with considerably less panache than he, that the cinema automatically projects worlds (in series). So might it be *for* a world? The computer, then, is simply *on* a world, as it tends to rise in separation from some referent, modeling and supplementing it. But enough phrase making, the crucial thing is to determine the nature of the machine.

Objects are never humans to a computer, nor are they faces or bodies. In this sense the computer breaks with those arts (painting, photography, cinema) that fixate upon the embodied human form – the face, but not always, the hand, but not always – and its proximal relation to a world, if not as their immediate subject matter then at least as the absolute horizon of their various aesthetic investments. The computer has not this same obsession. It aims not for man as an object. The reason is simple: because the computer is this object in and of itself.

Maybe this is why we do not cry at websites like we cry at the movies. Maybe it is why there is no "faciality" with the computer, why there is no concept of a celebrity star system (except ourselves), no characters or story (except our own), no notion of recognition and reversal, as Aristotle said of poetry. If the movie screen always directs toward, the computer screen always directs away. If at the movies you tilt your head back, with a computer you tilt in.

Profiles, not personas, drive the computer. Even as a certain kind of modern affect is in recession (following Jameson's famous argument about "the waning of affect" under postmodernity), there seems to be more affect today than ever before. Books are written on the subject. Conferences are devoted to it. The net is nothing if not the grand parade of personality profiles, wants and needs, projected egos, "second" selves and "second" lives. This is all true. So the triumph of affect is also its undoing. The waning of an older affective mode comes at the moment of its absolute rationalization into software. At the moment when something is perfected, it is dead. This is the condition of affect today online, and it is why the object of the computer is not a man: because its data is one.

Ultimately an additional step is necessary to explain the current reversal: *the computer is an anti-Ring of Gyges*. The scenario is inverted. The wearer of the ring is free to roam around in plain sight, while the world, invisible, retreats in absolute alterity. The world no longer indicates to us what it is. We indicate ourselves to it, and in doing so the world materializes in our image.

To be "informatically" present to the world, to experience the pleasure of the computer, one must be a sadist.[12] The penalties and rewards are clear. In contrast to the cinema, in order to be in a relation with the world informatically, one must erase the world, subjecting it to various forms of manipulation, preemption, modeling, and synthetic transformation. The computer takes our own superlative power over worlds as the condition of possibility for the creation of worlds. Our intense investment in worlds – our acute fact finding, our scanning and data mining, our spidering and extracting – is the precondition for how worlds are revealed. The promise is not one of revealing something as it is, but in simulating a thing so effectively that "what it is" becomes less and less necessary to speak about, not because it is gone for good, but because we have perfected a language *for* it.

Every object has its relations. As Alain Badiou writes, there are only bodies and languages.[13] It is necessary then to distinguish two grand domains which are, like fighting siblings, so much more different from one another strictly by virtue of being so intimately conjoined. *Media* and *mediation*, one might speak casually about one or the other without realizing the fundamental difference dividing them. It would not be necessary to accentuate the difference if others had not already mixed them up so awkwardly, or as is often the case failed to understand the subtlety in the first place. In reality these two systems are violently unconnected.

Recall the famous pronouncement from Friedrich Kittler that all technical media either store things, transmit things, or process things.[14] At the risk of sounding too juvenile, I will observe that this definition of media is particularly media-centric! By which is meant that Kittler first posits the existence of specific media technologies, say the *camera obscura* or the magic lantern, and then shows how they may or may not be furnished with special characteristics (sending, saving, or calculating). Technical media exist in various forms, and they do *x*, *y* or *z*. His is a revelatory story of objects and the qualities they carry. His is, in short, a hermeneutics of media devices as they appear after being pulled from the pit of history.

It leads to some delightful places, in particular the central thesis of the first section of his *Optical Media* lectures, in which he places the *camera obscura* and the magic lantern at the center of the history of all optical media. The *camera obscura* has a special relationship to linear perspective, the so-called "self-depiction of nature," and hence to Renaissance figures like Filippo Brunelleschi and Leon Battista Alberti. Because of this, it typifies for Kittler what Heidegger later would call "the age of the world picture." "[B]eing first constituted itself in the form of a representation (*Vorstellung*) in European modernity. Representational thinking delivered being as an object for a subject . . . [I]t can be said, following Heidegger's line of thought, that linear perspective and the *camera obscura* were precisely the media of this representation."[15] As a device for automatically recording images, the *camera obscura* functioned as a first-order simulation. It allowed reality to appear on a wall. By contrast, as a device for automatically reproducing or transmitting images, the magic lantern functioned as a second-order simulation. It allowed smaller images to appear larger on a wall. (The progression from first order to second order is appealing, and it sets Kittler up for a nice denouement: the film projector adopts the second-order quality of the magic lantern while adding a new digital simulation along the axis of time; television departs from the image entirely and instead goes for the symbolic space of language in which things are arranged in pixels and grids; and the computer annihilates the imaginary entirely, reverting back to that oldest of age-old media, writing.) Putting small, portable images up on a wall as large images, the essential task of the magic lantern, Kittler associates with Descartes' *cogito ergo sum*, wherein "the representation of the subject is re-presented to the subject once again as such."[16] Descartes' insistence in the *Meditations* that the philosopher must blot out the sun and sky and ball up his ears with wax illustrates for Kittler a particular model of mediation. Only the Cartesian self does what the magic lantern had already demonstrated: projects a representation, the thinking mind, back inward toward a previous representation, the self, and therefore (for Descartes at least) shores up the metaphysical relation. So what Heidegger saw as a vital spark in early-modern European man, his ability to cognize the world as a reflection, Descartes bent back into the folds of a baroque philosophy in which man reflects not on the primary data of nature but on the image of man himself. Copernicus, it seems, was wrong.

Still, Kittler's fixation on the media-centric nature of media puts him temporarily on some dangerous ground. For instance, this foolishness that "philosophy . . . has been necessarily unable to conceive of media as media," owing chiefly to the lack of imagination in a certain Aristotle, whose "ontology deals only with things, their matter and form, but not with relations between things in time and space. The very concept of a (physical) medium (tò metaxú) is relegated to his theory of sensorial perception (aisthesis)."[17] The insinuation here is bright and clear, why not state it unequivocally: Western philosophy since the Greeks has had no theory of mediation.[18]

Doubtless certain Greek philosophers had negative views regarding hypomnesis. Yet Kittler is reckless to suggest that the Greeks had no theory of mediation. The Greeks indubitably had an intimate understanding of the physicality of transmission and message sending (Hermes). They differentiated between mediation as immanence and mediation as expression (Iris versus Hermes). They understood the mediation of poetry via the Muses and their techne. They understood the mediation of bodies through the "middle loving" Aphrodite. They even understood swarming and networked presence (in the incontinent mediating forms of the Eumenides who pursued Orestes in order to "process" him at the procès of Athena). Thus we need only look a little bit further to shed this rather vulgar, consumer-electronics view of media, and instead graduate into the deep history of media as modes of mediation, a task that with a bit of luck will be accomplished presently vespere et mane.

Realizing the danger, Kittler retreats slightly from the more extreme argument. He explains that, while Aristotle might exclude media from his theory of matter and form, he doesn't act likewise in his discussion of human perception. "Aristotle, however, speaks of two elements, namely air and water, as of two 'betweens.' In other words, he is the first to turn a common Greek preposition – *metaxú*, between – into a philosophical noun or concept: *tò metaxú*, the medium. 'In the middle' of absence and presence, farness and nearness, being and soul, there exists no nothing any more, but a mediatic relation. *Es gibt Medien*, we could say."[19] Hence even if Aristotle does not discuss mediation when he talks about hylomorphism and ontology, he nevertheless inaugurates philosophy's centuries-long relationship to media via a discussion of the human senses. The missing interlocutor here is Bernard Stiegler, who has perhaps more clearly than anyone since Heidegger framed the intimate co-construction of technology and being.

All of this now in the light of day, I am in a position to identify more clearly the conservatism of Kittler, who on this point finds a confrere in Marshall McLuhan. By conservative I mean the claim that *techne* is substrate and only substrate. For Kittler and McLuhan alike, media mean hypomnesis. They define media via the externalization of man into objects. Hence a fundamentally conservative dichotomy is inaugurated – which to be clear was in Plato before it was in Aristotle – between the good and balanced human specimen and the dead junk of the hypomnemata. Contrast this with an alternate philosophical tradition that views *techne* as technique, art, habitus, ethos, or lived practice. Such an alternate tradition is what was alluded to previously, through the contrast between media (as objects or substrates) and practices of mediation (as middles or interfaces). Indeed it is ironic that Kittler hews so closely to Heidegger, as Heidegger was one of the philosophers who best understood both aspects of *techne*.

We are not finished yet however. For Kittler also harbors a deep-seated interest in another ancient yearning of philosophy, one which is as old as it is powerful. It is the desire to reduce the many to the one. In *Optical Media*, during his discussion of film Kittler stresses the way in which Étienne-Jules Marey was committed to a single camera, thereby reducing many devices to a single apparatus: "By holding tight to the unifying, linearizing power of writing paper, Marey always only needed one single piece of equipment, while Muybridge had to position 12 different cameras. The task, therefore, was to dispose of 11 cameras and still be able to supply serial photographs. In the process, Colt's good old revolver was once again honored, as it had also reduced the need for six pistols down to one."[20] Later, in his discussion of television he says something similar: "In contrast to film, therefore, the problem of television from the very beginning was how to make a single channel dimension from two image dimensions, and how to make a single time variable from convertible surfaces."[21] And again later in the albeit short discussion of computers: "[C]omputers represent the successful reduction of all dimensions to zero."[22] (Given what I intend to argue in a future essay addressed to the fundamental "parallelity" of the image, it will be possible to demonstrate that the computer is never the product of a reduction from two to one, or from the multiple to the zero, but in fact the reverse, for the computer belongs to that long aesthetic tradition that derives all of its energy from a fission of the one dividing into the multiple.[23]) The reduction of the many to the one is symptomatic, not only of a latent politics lurking within the Kittlerian corpus, but also, more simply, of the aforementioned prioritization of the object over the middle. A philosophy of mediation will tend to proliferate multiplicity; a philosophy of media will tend to agglomerate difference into reified objects. Perhaps this is why Kittler, although notable among his peers for an intrepid willingness to write on computers, never fully theorized digital media as much as other media technologies and platforms, for where is the object of distributed networks located, where is a rhizome, where is software? For Kittler, alas, "there is no software."[24]

I applaud Kittler, though, for his understanding of the relation between computers and the optical. Many scholars today continue to classify the computer as another installment in the long march of visual culture. As Kittler makes clear, such a position is totally wrong. Subsequent to television, which began a retreat away from optical media and a return to the symbolic in the form of signal codification, the computer consummates the retreat from the realm of the imaginary to the purely symbolic realm of writing. "In contrast to film, television was already no longer optics," he writes. "Digital image processing thus ultimately represents the liquidation of this last remainder of the imaginary. The reason is simple: computers, as they have existed since the World War II, are not designed for image-processing at all."[25]

Nevertheless the archive extends its influence over Kittler's thinking. For he thinks of technical media primarily in terms of artifacts, artifacts for storage, transmission, or processing. But what if we were to take the ultimate step and pose the question of media in reverse? What if we refuse to embark from the premise of "technical media" and instead begin from the perspective of their supposed predicates: storing, transmitting, and processing? With the verbal nouns at the helm, a new set of possibilities appears. These are modes of mediation, not media per se. The shift is slight but crucial. The mode of storage appears instantly within its own illumination; the mode of transmitting returns from a far-off place; the mode of processing wells up like a flood of pure energy.

Gilles Deleuze has suggested as much in his work. In the essay "What Is a *Dispositif*?" Deleuze writes that one should not focus so much on devices or apparatuses as such and more on the physical systems of power they mobilize, that is, more on curves of visibility and lines of force. "These apparatuses, then, are composed of the following elements: lines of visibility and enunciation, lines of force, lines of subjectification, lines of splitting, breakage, fracture, all of which crisscross and mingle together, some lines reproducing or giving rise to others, by means of variations or even changes in the way they are grouped."[26] When Kittler elevates substrates and apparatuses over modes of mediation, he forfeits an interest in techniques in favor of an interest in objects. A middle – a compromise, a translation, a corruption, a revelation, a certainty, an infuriation, a touch, a flux – is not a medium, by virtue of it not being a technical media device.

What is the computer, then, as a mode of mediation? Cavell, and he is not the only one simply the most convenient, speaks of the possibility of a medium. The possibility of a medium stands in intimate relation to what a medium is, that is to say, the definition of whatever medium is in question. Thus when one asks "What is the possibility of video?" one is in the same breath asking "What is the definition of video?" Yet the computer occupies an uneasy position in relation to both definition and possibility, for in many cases the very words that people use to address the question of the computer are those selfsame words "definition" and "possibility." One hears stories about computers being "definitional" machines: not only does computer code operate through the definitions of states and state changes, but computers themselves are those special machines that nominalize the world, that define and model its behavior using variables and functions. Likewise one hears stories about computers being "possibility" machines: they operate not through vague estimations of practice, but through hard, machinic possibilities of truth or falsehood, openness or closedness, on or off. So I suggest that these terms "definition" and "possibility" might do more harm than good if our aim is to understand the machine and how it works. How can we determine the possibility of new media if new media are nothing but possibility machines? How can we define them if they are already cast from the mold of definition? To adopt a shorthand, one might summarize this state of affairs by asserting that the computer has hitherto been understood in terms of metaphysics. That is to say, when people speak about the computer as an "essencing machine" what they really mean is that computers simulate ontologies, they define horizons of possibility. This is the terrain of metaphysics. These sorts of definitions can be found in Lev Manovich, Janet Murray, and all across the discourse on new media today. The notion is that one must define the medium with reference to a specific "language" or set of essential formal qualities, which then, following the metaphysical logic, manifest in the world a number of instances or effects. (One of the shortcomings of this approach, which I will not delve into very deeply here, is the problem of essentialism, that is to say, the notion that new media objects are a priori a certain way, and it is merely the job of the critic to examine them, and extract the universal laws or languages that constitute their proper functioning in the world; my elders in the anti-essentialist critical tradition – from Homi Bhabha to Donna Haraway and beyond – have rightfully pointed out how this leads eventually to a number of political and theoretical problems, least of which being that it forecloses on contingency and historicity, two things that turn out to be quite desirable indeed.)[27]

Inoffensive thus far, however the story becomes more complicated once we acknowledge that the computer is dramatically unlike other media. Instead of facilitating the metaphysical arrangement, the computer does something quite different: it simulates the metaphysical arrangement. In short, the computer does not remediate other physical media, it remediates metaphysics itself (and hence should be more correctly labeled a metaphysical medium). I shall refrain from saying it remediates mediation itself, but the temptation exists. The metaphysical "medium" of essences and instances is fundamentally dead today. And because it is dead, the medium of essences and instances reemerges in a new mediatic form, the computer. Informatic machines do not *participate* in the worldly logic of essences and instances, they simulate it. For example, principles like disposability and planned obsolescence, on the one hand, seem to occlude age-old metaphysical problems about the persistence of essential identity in the form of universals or transcendents. Quite frankly, the metaphysical questions are simply not the interesting ones to ask in the face of all this junk. But on the other hand, within the logic of the machine one sees little more than an effigy for, and an undead persistence of, these same metaphysical principles. As was said previously regarding affect, things always reach their perfection in death.

The remediation argument (handed down from McLuhan and his followers including Kittler) is so full of holes that it is probably best to toss it wholesale. So what to do with the notion of remediating metaphysics itself? If any hope may be found for the remediation theory, it is in the "itself." Television does not simply remediate film, it remediates film *itself.* The important issue is not that this or that film is scanned and broadcast as the "content" of television (this being one version of McLuhan's remediation argument). The important issue is that television incorporates film itself, that is, it incorporates the entire, essential cinematic condition.

Hypotheses governing remediation are quickly put to the test. Kittler's amazing discussion of time axis manipulation in recorded sound is instructive on this point.[28] Recorded sound may remediate performed music, but what is being remediated when a musician plays magnetic tape backward and hears for the first time a true sonic reversal (not simply the reversal of phonemes)? Or consider the computer. A computer might remediate text and image. But what about a computer crash? What is being remediated at that moment? It can't be text or image anymore, for they are not subject to crashes of this variety. So is a computer crash an example of non-media? In short, the remediation hypothesis leads very quickly to a feedback loop in which much of what we consider to be media are in fact reclassified as non-media, thereby putting into question the suitability of the original hypothesis.

A brief reference to object-oriented programming will help illustrate the problems surrounding the remediation of metaphysics itself. The metaphysico-Platonic logic of object-oriented systems is awe inspiring, particularly the way in which classes (forms) define objects (instantiated things): classes are programmer-defined templates, they are (usually) static and state in abstract terms how objects define data types and process data; objects are instances of classes, they are created in the image of a class, they persist for finite amounts of time and eventually are destroyed. On the one hand an idea, on the other a body. On the one hand an essence, on the other an instance. On the one hand the ontological, on the other the ontical.

Cinema so captured the twentieth-century imagination that it is common to assume that other media are also at root cinematic. And since the cinema is, in general, an ontology (in particular it is a phenomenology), it seems logical to assume that other media are ontological in the same way. The computer however, is not *of* an ontological condition, it is *on* that condition. It does not facilitate or make reference to an arrangement of being, it remediates the very conditions of being itself. If I may be so crude: the medium of the computer is being. But one must take this in an entirely unglamorous way. It is not to say that the computer is the ontological actor par excellence, that it marks the way for some cyborg *Dasein* of the future. No, the point is that the computer has so degraded the ontological plane, that it may reduce and simulate it using the simple principles of logical relation. Being is its object, not its experience. And if being is merely its object, we ought to look elsewhere to try to understand its experience.

The computer instantiates a practice not a presence, an effect not an object. In other words, *if cinema is, in general, an ontology, the computer is, in general, an ethic.* Perhaps a useful way to understand the distinction is to differentiate between a language and a calculus. A language operates at the level of description and reference. To encode the world, this is the primary goal of language. (Of course one might also speak about the autonomous space of language, in for example textuality, as a space of interconnection and deferral of meaning, and so on.) A calculus, on the other hand, operates at the level of computation and process. To do something to the world – or if you like to simulate doing something to the world – this is the primary goal of a calculus. With a calculus, one speaks of a system of reasoning, an executable machine that can work through a problem, step by step. The difference between the two, in one aspect, is that a calculus implies a method, whereas a language does not.

I make a distinction between an ethic, which describes general principles for practice, and the realm of the ethical, which defines such general principles for practice within the context of a specifically human relationship to moral conceptions of the good. So to say that the computer is in general an ethic is *not* to say that computers are "ethical." Note therefore that mine is not a personification of the machine, but rather an anti-anthropocentrism of the realm of practice. And I will always defend the unpopular notion that, in the end, machines really have no need for humans at all (just in the same way that the Real has no need for us, but we have a horrifying need for it). Yet in actual fact the machine does have an anthropocentric relation, and this is where one might speak to the question of a computer ethic. As an ethic, the computer takes our action in the world as such as the condition of the world's expression. So in saying practice, I am really indicating a relationship of command. The machine is an ethic because it is premised on the notion that objects are subject to definition and manipulation according to a set of principles for action. The matter at hand is not that of coming to know a world, but rather that of how specific, abstract definitions are executed to form a world.

Ontology often receives top billing in questions philosophical, even in cases when its hegemony is not warranted. So let me restate the argument: the computer has hitherto been defined ontologically; but this approach (using the ontological concepts of possibility and definition) is dubious because the computer itself is already a matter of possibility and definition; thus if the computer might better be understood in terms of a practice or a set of executions or actions in relation to a world, the proper branch of philosophy that one should turn to is ethics or pragmatics, not ontology or metaphysics; as an ethics, the computer takes our execution of the world as the condition of the world's expression. And this is the interface effect again, only in different language: the computer is not an object, or a creator of objects, it is a process or active threshold mediating between two states.

Neither an object nor a creator of objects – but where does this get us? First, beyond the response to Kittler, we can now rekindle the response to Manovich begun at the outset. The main difficulty with a book like *The Language of New Media*, for all its strength, is not simply that it participates in the various squabbles over this or that formal detail. Are games fundamentally about play or about narrative? What has greater semiotic priority, code or interface? In the end these territorial skirmishes do not interest me much. The main difficulty is the simple premise of the book, that new media may be defined via reference to a foundational set of formal qualities, and that these qualities form a coherent language that may be identified across all sorts of new media objects, and above all that the qualities may be read, and may be interpreted. This is what was called, many years ago, structuralism. Let me be clear, it is not so much that these sorts of books are misguided (and not so much to pick on Manovich, for there are scores of other texts that do similar work; his simply is one of the earliest and most accomplished examples), but that their conclusions are unappetizing. This is the crux of the matter: they contain no injunction. They talk more about objects and operations than practices and effects. The problem is not formal definition – for after all I am willing to participate in such a project, suggesting for example that with informatic machines we must fundamentally come to terms with the problem of action. The sticking point is that, in this instance, the use of formalism as a method does not ultimately conform most faithfully to the subject at hand. That is, if the computer *were* a formal medium, then perhaps our analysis of it could be too. But my position is that it is not exclusively or even predominantly formal. So in a certain sense, Manovich is, shall we say, slightly more avant-garde, performing an "intervention," while my call is much more conservative. If the language (of new media) is really an executable language and not simply a natural one, then would it not make sense for one's critical appraisal to be in step with that same notion of executability? So when I say that these other authors' conclusions are unappetizing it should be taken in the most mundane sense: that the current discourse on "excitable" machines – to put it bluntly – is not that exciting. In other words, if computers must be understood in terms of an ethics (those who wish instead to call it a politics should do so), then the discourse produced about them must also fulfill various ethical and political expectations. Else what is the good?

1 The Unworkable Interface

Interface as Method

Interfaces are back, or perhaps they never left. The familiar Socratic conceit, from the *Phaedrus*, of communication as the process of writing directly on the soul of the other has, since the 1980s and 1990s, returned to center stage in the discourse around culture and media. The catoptrics of the society of the spectacle is now the dioptrics of the society of control. Reflective surfaces have been overthrown by transparent thresholds. The metal detector arch, or the graphics frustum, or the Unix socket – these are the new emblems of the age.

Frames, windows, doors, and other thresholds are those transparent devices that achieve more the less they do: for every moment of virtuosic immersion and connectivity, for every moment of volumetric delivery, of inopacity, the threshold becomes one notch more invisible, one notch more inoperable. As technology, the more a dioptric device erases the traces of its own functioning (in actually delivering the thing represented beyond), the more it succeeds in its functional mandate; yet this very achievement undercuts the ultimate goal: the more intuitive a device becomes, the more it risks falling out of media altogether, becoming as naturalized as air or as common as dirt. To succeed, then, is at best self-deception and at worst self-annihilation. One must work hard to cast the glow of unwork. Operability engenders inoperability.

But curiously this is not a chronological, spatial, or even semiotic relation. It is primarily a systemic relation, as Michel

Serres rightly observed in his meditation on functional "along-sidedness": "Systems work because they don't work. Non-functionality remains essential for functionality. This can be formalized: pretend there are two stations exchanging messages through a channel. If the exchange succeeds – if it is perfect, optimal, immediate – then the relation erases itself. But if the relation remains there, if it exists, it's because the exchange has failed. It is nothing but mediation. The relation is a non-relation."[1] Thus since Plato, we have been wrestling with the grand choice: (1) mediation as the process of imminent if not immediate realization of the other (and thus at the same time the self), or (2) as Serres' dialectical position suggests, mediation as the irreducible disintegration of self and other into contradiction.[2] Representation is either clear or complicated, either inherent or extrinsic, either beautiful or deceptive, either already known or endlessly interpretable. In short, either Iris or Hermes. Without wishing to upend this neat and tidy formulation, it is still useful to focus on the contemporary moment to see if something slightly different is going on, or, at the very least to "prove" the seemingly already known through close analysis of some actual cultural artifacts.

Either Iris or Hermes – but what does this mean for intellectual exploration? Before tackling the interface directly, I would like to interject a brief prefatory announcement on methodology. To the extent that the present project is allegorical in nature, it might be useful to, as it were, subtend the process of allegorical reading in the age of ludic capitalism with some elaboration as to how or why it might be possible to perform such a reading in the first place. In former times, it was generally passable to appeal to some legitimizing methodological foundation – usually Marx or Freud or some combination thereof – in order to prove the efficacy, and indeed the political potency, of one's critical maneuverings. This is not to suggest that those sources are no longer viable, quite the opposite, since power typically grows with claims of obsolescence; even today Marx's death-drive persists under the pseudonyms of Antonio Negri, Paolo Virno, or McKenzie Wark, just as a generation ago it persisted under Jean-Joseph

Goux or Guy Debord. Yet somehow today the unfashionable sheen, and indeed perceived illegitimacy, of the critical tradition inherited from the middle of the nineteenth century and the beginning of the twentieth, with Marx and Freud standing as two key figures in this tradition but certainly not encompassing all of it, makes it difficult to rally around the red flag of desire in the same way as before. Today the form of Marxism in common circulation is still the antiseptic one invented a generation ago by Louis Althusser: Marx may be dissected with rubber gloves, the rational kernel of his thought cut out and extruded into some form of scientific discourse of analysis – call it critique or what have you. On the other front, to mention psychoanalysis these days generally earns a smirk if not a condescending giggle, a wholesale transformation from the middle of the twentieth century in which Freudianisms of various shapes and sizes saturated the popular imagination. Realizing this, many have turned elsewhere for methodological inspiration.

I acknowledge such shifts in the critical landscape. Nevertheless I also maintain that Marx and Freud still allow us the ability to do two important things: (1) provide an account of the so-called depth model of interpretation; (2) provide an account of how and why something appears in the form of its opposite. In our times, so distressed on all sides by the arrival of neoliberal economism, these two things together still constitute the core act of critique. So for the moment Marx and Freud remain useful, if not absolutely elemental, despite a certain amount of antiseptic neutering.

Nevertheless times have changed, have they not? The social and economic conditions today are different from what they were one hundred or one hundred and fifty years ago. Writers from Manuel Castells to Alan Liu to Luc Boltanski have described a new socio-economic landscape, one in which flexibility, play, creativity, and immaterial labor – call it ludic capitalism – have taken over from the old concepts of discipline, hierarchy, bureaucracy, and muscle. In particular, two historical trends stand out as essential in this new play economy. The first is a return to romanticism, from which today's concept of play receives an eternal endowment. Friedrich Schiller's *On the Aesthetic Education of Man* is emblematic in this regard. In it, the philosopher uses dialectical logic to arrive at the concept of the play-drive, the object of which is man's "living form." This notion of play is one of abundance and creation, of pure unsullied authenticity, of a childlike, tinkering vitality perennially springing forth from the core of that which is most human. More recently one hears this same refrain in Johan Huizinga's book on play *Homo Ludens* (which has been cited widely across the political spectrum, from French Situationists to social conservatives), or even in the work of the poststructuralists, often so hostile to other seemingly "uninterrogated" concepts.[3]

Game theory, ecology, systems theory, information theory, behaviorism – these many scientific disciplines point to the second element, that of cybernetics. While in development during and before the Second World War, cybernetics seemed to gel rapidly in 1947 or 1948, soon becoming a new dominant. With cybernetics, the notion of play adopts a special interest in homeostasis and systemic interaction. The world's entities are no longer contained and contextless but are forever operating within ecosystems of interplay and correspondence. This is a notion of play centered on economic flows and balances, multilateral associations between things, a resolution of complex systemic relationships via mutual experimenting, mutual compromise, mutual engagement. Thus, nowadays, one "plays around" with a problem in order to find a workable solution. (Recall the dramatic difference in language between this and Descartes' "On Method" or other key works of modern, positivistic rationality.)

Romanticism and cybernetic systems theory: play today is a synthesis of these two influences. If the emblematic profession for the former is poetry, the latter is design. The one is expressive, consummated in an instant; the other is iterative, extending in all directions. The two became inextricably fused during the second half of the twentieth century, subsumed within the contemporary concept of play. Thus what Debord called the "juridico-geometric" nature of games is not entirely complete.[4] He understood the ingredient of systemic interaction well enough, but he understated the romantic ingredient.

Today's play might better be described as a sort of "juridico-geometric sublime." Witness the Web itself, which exhibits all three elements: the universal laws of protocological exchange, sprawling across complex topologies of aggregation and dissemination, and resulting in the awesome forces of "emergent" vitality. This is what romantico-cybernetic play means. Today's ludic capitalist is therefore the consummate poet-designer, forever coaxing new value out of raw, systemic interactions (consider the example of Google). And all the rest has changed to follow the same rubric: labor itself is now play, just as play becomes more and more laborious; or consider the model of the market, in which the invisible hand of play intervenes to assess and resolve all contradiction, and is thought to model all phenomena, from energy futures markets, to the "market" of representational democracy, to haggling over pollution credits, to auctions of the electromagnetic spectrum, to all manner of supercharged speculation in the art world. Play is the thing that overcomes systemic contradiction but always via recourse to that special, ineffable thing that makes us most human. It is, as it were, *a melodrama of the rhizome.*

Enlisting these types of periodization arguments, some point out that as history changes so too must change the act of reading. Thus, the argument goes, as neoliberal economism leverages the ludic flexibility of networks, so too must the critic resort to new methodologies of scanning, playing, sampling, parsing, and recombining. The critic might then be better off as a sort of remix artist, a disc jockey of the mind.

Maybe so. But while the forces of ludic distraction are many, they coalesce around one clarion call: be more like us. To follow such a call and label it nature serves merely to reify what is fundamentally a historical relation. The new ludic economy is in fact a call for violent renovation of the social fabric from top to bottom using the most nefarious techniques available. That today it comes under the name of Google or Monsanto is a mere footnote.

Addressing this larger reality, I will be the first to admit that the present methodology is not particularly rhizomatic or playful in spirit, for the spirit of play and rhizomatic revolution have been deflated in recent years. It is instead that of a material and semiotic "close reading," aspiring not to reenact the historical relation (the new economy) but to identify the relation itself as historical. In other words, not to reenact the interface, much less to "define" it, *but to identify the interface itself as historical.* What I hope this produces is a perspective on how cultural production and the socio-historical situation take form as they are interfaced together. Or if that is too much jargon: what form art and politics take. If this will pass as an adequate syncretism of Freud and Marx, with a few necessary detours nevertheless back to Gilles Deleuze and elsewhere, then so be it.[5]

Indeed the ultimate task in this chapter is not simply to illustrate the present cocktail of methodological influences necessary to analyze today's digital interfaces. That would be to put the cart before the horse. The ultimate task is to reveal that *this methodological cocktail is itself an interface.* Or more precisely, it is to show that the interface itself, as a "control allegory," indicates the way toward a specific methodological stance. The interface asks a question and, in so doing, suggests an answer.

Two Interfaces

New media foreground the interface like never before. Screens of all shapes and sizes tend to come to mind: computer screens, ATM kiosks, phone keypads, and so on. This is what Vilém Flusser called simply a "significant surface," meaning a two-dimensional plane with meaning embedded in it or delivered through it. There is even a particular vernacular adopted to describe or evaluate such significant surfaces. We say "they are user-friendly," or "they are not user-friendly." "They are intuitive" or "they are not intuitive."

Still, it is also quite common to understand interfaces less as a surface but as a doorway or window. This is the language of thresholds and transitions already evoked at the start of the chapter. Following this position, an interface is not something that appears before you but rather is a gateway that opens up and allows passage to some place beyond. Larger twentieth-century trends around information science, systems theory, and cybernetics add more to the story. The notion of the interface becomes very important for example in the science of cybernetics, for it is the place where flesh meets metal or, in the case of systems theory, the interface is the place where information moves from one entity to another, from one node to another within the system.

Often interfaces are assumed to be synonymous with media itself. But what would it mean to say that "interface" and "media" are two names for the same thing? The answer is found in the *remediation* or *layer model* of media, broached already in the introduction, wherein media are essentially nothing but formal containers housing other pieces of media. This is a claim most clearly elaborated on the opening pages of Marshall McLuhan's *Understanding Media*. McLuhan liked to articulate this claim in terms of media history: a new medium is invented, and as such its role is as a container for a previous media format. So, film is invented at the tail end of the nineteenth century as a container for photography, music, and various theatrical formats like vaudeville. What is video but a container for film. What is the Web but a container for text, image, video clips, and so on. Like the layers of an onion, one format encircles another, and it is media all the way down. This definition is well-established today, and it is a very short leap from there to the idea of interface, for the interface becomes the point of transition between different mediatic layers within any nested system. The interface is an "agitation" or generative friction between different formats. In computer science, this happens very literally; an "interface" is the name given to the way in which one glob of code can interact with another. Since any given format finds its identity merely in the fact that it is a container for another format, the concept of interface and medium quickly collapse into one and the same thing.

Nevertheless, is this the entire story of the interface? The parochialism of those who fetishize screen-based media suggests that something else is going on too. If the remediation argument has any purchase at all, it would be shortsighted to limit the scope of one's analysis to a single medium or indeed a single aggregation under the banner of something like "the digital." The notion of thresholds would warn against it. Thus a classical source, selected for its generic quality, not its specificity, is now appropriate. How does Hesiod begin his song?

> The everlasting immortals . . .
> It was they who once taught Hesiod his splendid singing . . .
> They told me to sing the race of the blessed gods everlasting,
> but always to put themselves at the beginning and end of my
>   singing.[6]

Endless similar formulations are found in classical poetry, from Homer and beyond: "Sing in me Muse, and through me tell the story of . . ." The poet does not so much originate his own song as serve as a conduit for divine expression received from without. The poet is, in this sense, wrapped up by the Muse, or as Socrates puts it in the *Phaedrus*, possessed. "To put themselves at the beginning and end" – I suggest that this is our first real clue as to what an interface is.

All media evoke similar liminal transition moments in which the outside is evoked in order that the inside may take place. In the case of the classical poet, what is the outside? It is the Muse, the divine source, which is first evoked and praised, in order for the outside to possess the inside. Once possessed by the outside, the poet sings and the story transpires.

Needless to say such observations are not limited to the classical context. Prefatory evocations of the form "once upon a time" are common across media formats. The French author François Dagognet describes it thus: "The interface . . . consists essentially of an area of choice. It both separates and mixes the two worlds that meet together there, that run into it. It becomes a fertile nexus."[7] Dagognet presents the expected themes of thresholds, doorways, and windows. But he complicates the story a little bit in admitting that there are complex things that take place inside that threshold; the interface is not simple and transparent but a "fertile nexus." He is more Flusser and less McLuhan.[8] The interface for Dagognet is a special place with its own autonomy, its own ability to generate new results and consequences. It is an "area of choice" between the Muse and the poet, between the divine and the mortal, between the edge and the center.

Dagognet articulates the basic question, even if he doesn't provide the most useful answer: what is an edge and what is a center? Where does the image end and the frame begin? This is something with which artists have played for generations. Digital media are exceptionally good at artifice and often the challenge comes in maintaining the distinction between edge and center, a distinction that threatens to collapse at any point like a house of cards. For example, the difference is entirely artificial between legible ASCII text, on a Web page, for example, and ASCII text used in HTML markup on that same page. It is a matter of syntactic techniques of encoding. One imposes a certain linguistic and stylistic construct in order to create these artificial differentiations. Technically speaking, the artificial distinction is the case all the way down: there is no *essential* difference between data and algorithm, the differentiation is purely artificial. The interface is this state of "being on the boundary." It is that moment where one significant material is understood as distinct from another significant material. In other words, an interface is not a thing, an interface is always an effect. It is always a process or a translation. Again Dagognet: a fertile nexus.

To distill these observations into something of a slogan, one might say that *the edges of art always make reference to the medium itself.*

However this is a common claim is it not, particularly within discourse around modernism? But it is possible to expand the notion more broadly so that it applies to the act of mediation in general. Homer invokes the Muse, the literal form of poetry, in order to enact and embody that same divine form. But even in the song of the poem itself, Homer turns away from the narrative structure, in an apostrophe, to speak to a character as if he were an object of direct address: "And you, Atrides . . .," "and you, Achilles."

Objects of address appear in many different ways in art, and are treated differently depending on the medium. To develop this thread further, I turn to the first of two case studies.

Figure 1.1. Norman Rockwell, "Triple Self-Portrait," *The Saturday Evening Post*, February 13, 1960. Printed by permission of the Norman Rockwell Family Agency; Book Rights Copyright © 1960 The Norman Rockwell Family Entities.

Norman Rockwell's "Triple Self-Portrait" (1960) presents a dazzling array of various interfaces (Fig. 1.1). It is, at root, a meditation on the interface itself. The portrait of the artist appears in the image, only redoubled and multiplied a few times over. But the illustration is not a perfect system of representation. There is a circulation of coherence within the image that gestures toward the outside, while ultimately remaining afraid of it. Three portraits immediately appear:

(1) the portrait of an artist sitting on a stool, (2) the artist's reflection in the mirror, and (3) the half-finished picture on the canvas. Yet the image does not terminate there, as additional layers supplement the three obvious ones: (4) a prototypical interface of early sketches on the top left of the canvas, serving as a prehistory of malformed image production, (5) on the top right, an array of self-portraits by European masters that provide the artist some inspiration, and (6) a hefty signature of the (real) artist at center right, craftily embedded inside the image, inside another image.

Unusual side effects emerge from such a complicated circulation of images and meta-images. First, the artist paints in front of an off-white sweep wall, not unlike the antiseptic, white nowhere land that would later become a staple of science fiction films like *THX 1138* or *The Matrix*. Inside this off-white nowhere land, there appears to be no visible outside – no landscape at all – to locate or orient the artist's coherent circulation of image production. But second, and more important, is the dramatic difference in representational and indeed moral and spiritual vitality between the image in the mirror and the picture on the canvas. The image in the mirror is presented as a technical or machinic image, while the picture on the canvas is a subjective, expressive image. In the mirror, the artist is bedraggled, dazzled behind two opaque eyeglass lenses, performing the rote tasks of his vocation (and evidently not entirely thrilled about it). On the canvas, instead, is a perfected, special version of himself. His vision is corrected in the canvas world. His pipe no longer sags but shoots up in a jaunty appeal. Even the lines on the artist's brow lose their foreboding on canvas, signifying instead the soft wisdom of an elder. Other dissimilarities abound, particularly the twofold growth in size and the lack of color in the canvas image, which while seemingly more perfect is ultimately muted and impoverished. But there is a fourth layer of this interface, the "quadruplicate" supplement to the triple self-portrait: the illustration itself. It is also an interface, this time between us and the magazine cover. This is typically the level of the interface that is most invisible, particularly within the format of middlebrow kitsch of which Rockwell is a master. The fact that this is a self-conscious self-portrait also assists in making that fourth level invisible because all the viewer's energies that might have been reserved for tackling those difficult "meta" questions about reflections and layers and reflexive circulation of meaning are exercised to exhaustion before they have the opportunity to interrogate the frame of the illustration itself.

Glib assessments of the illustration would describe it as mere semiotic catharsis, an image designed to keep the viewer's eye from straying too far afield, while at the same time avoiding any responsibility of thinking the image as such. The image claims to address the viewer's concerns within the content of the image (within what should be called by its proper name, the *diegetic* space of the image). But it only raises these concerns so that they may be held in suspension. In a larger sense, this is the same semiotic labor that is performed by genre forms in general, as well as kitsch, baroque, and other modes of visceral expression: to implant in the viewer the desires they thought they wanted to begin with, and then to fulfill every craving of that same artificial desire. Artificial desire – can there be any other kind?

Have we avoided the question though? Again, what is an edge and what is a center? Is Rockwell evoking the Muse or simply suspending her? Where exactly is the line between the text and the paratext? The best way to answer these questions is not to point to a set of entities in the image, pronouncing proudly that these five or six details are textual, while those seven or eight others are paratextual. Instead, one must always return to the following notion: an interface is not a thing; an interface is an effect. (This being the same refrain sung throughout the book, not media but mediation.) One must look at local relationships within the image and ask how such relationships create an externalization, an incoherence, an edging, or a framing? Or in reverse: how does this other specific local relationship within the apparatus succeed in creating a coherence, a centering, a localization? But what does this mean? Project yourself into Rockwell's image. There exists a diegetic circuit between the artist, the mirror, and the canvas. The circuit is a circulation of intensity. Nevertheless, this does not prohibit the viewer from going outside the circuit. The stress here is that one must always think about the image as a process, rather than as a set of discrete, immutable items. The paratextual (or alternately, the nondiegetic) is in this sense merely the process that goes by the name of outering, of exteriority.

To laugh at the joke, intimated but never consummated by Rockwell's triple self-portrait, one should turn to the satire produced a few years later by Richard Williams for *Mad* magazine (Fig. 1.2).[9] The humor comes from *Mad*'s trickster mascot.

Figure 1.2. Richard A. Williams, "Untitled (Alfred E. Neuman Self-Portrait)." Source: Mark Evanier, *Mad Art* (New York: Watson-Guptill, 2002), front cover.

Being an artist of such great talent, he not only paints a portrait of himself but does so from the viewer's subjective vantage point. In this sense, the interface is a kind of semiotic short circuit.

But unlike Rockwell's avatar, *Mad*'s mascot has no concern for making himself look better in art, only to make himself appear more clever. There is no anxiety in this image. There is no pipe; there are no glasses. It is in color. It is the same head, only bigger. And of course, it is the view of the back of the head, not the face, front and forward. The mode of address is now the core of the image: Rockwell's eyes were glazed, but the *Mad* mascot here is quite clearly addressing the viewer. There is an intensity of circulation within Rockwell's image, whereby each added layer puts a curve into the viewer's gaze, always gravitating centripetally toward the middle. But in Williams' *Mad* satire those circular coherences are replaced by three orthogonal spikes that break the image apart: (1) the face in the mirror looks orthogonally outward at the external viewer, (2) the seated figure looks orthogonally inward and not at the mirror as the laws of optics would dictate, and likewise (3) the canvas portrait faces orthogonally inward, mimicking the look of the big orthogonal Other, the external viewer.

Every ounce of energy within the image is aimed at its own externalization. Looking back at the history of art-making, one remembers that addressing the viewer is a very special mode of representation that is often saved or segregated or cast off and reserved for special occasions. It appears in debased forms like pornography, or folk forms like the home video, or marginalized political forms like Brechtian theater, or forms of ideological interpellation like the nightly news. Direct address is always treated in a special way. Narrative forms, which are still dominant in many media, almost entirely prohibit it. For example, by the 1930s in film, direct address is something that cannot be done, at least within the confines of classical Hollywood form. It becomes quite literally a sign of the avant-garde. Yet *Mad*'s fourth interface, the direct address of the image itself, is included as part of the frame. It is entirely folded into the logic of the image. The gargantuan head on the canvas, in turning away, is in reality turning toward, bringing the edge into the center.

Considering them side by side, Rockwell and *Mad* present two ways of thinking about the same problem. In the first is an interface that addresses itself to the theme of the interface; Rockwell's is an image that addresses image-making in general. But it answers the problem of the interface through the neurosis of repression. In orienting itself toward interfaces, it suggests simultaneously that interfaces don't exist. It puts the stress on a coherent, closed, abstract aesthetic world. On the other hand, the second image solves the problem of the interface through the psychosis of schizophrenia. It returns forever to the original trauma of the interface itself. Reveling in the disorientation of shattered coherence, the second image makes no attempt to hide the interface. Instead, the orthogonal axis of concern, lancing outward from the image, seizes the viewer. In it, the logic of the image disassembles into incoherence. So the tension between these two images is that of coherence versus incoherence, of centers creating an autonomous logic versus edges creating a logic of flows, transformations, movement, process, and lines of flight. The edges are firmly evoked in the second image. They are dissolved in the first.

On the one hand Rockwell's image is internally consistent. It is an interface that works. The interface has a logic that may be known and articulated by the interface itself. It works; it works *well*.

Mad's image, on the other hand, is an image that doesn't work. It is an interface that is unstable. It is, as Maurice Blanchot or Jean-Luc Nancy might say, *désoeuvré* – nonworking, unproductive, inoperative, unworkable.

Intraface

Earlier discussions of interfaces as doors or windows now reveal their limitations. One must transgress the threshold, as it were, of the threshold theory of the interface. A window testifies that it imposes no mode of representation on that which passes through it. A doorway says something similar, only it complicates the formula slightly by admitting that it may be *closed* from time to time, impeding or even blocking the passengers within. The discourse is thus forever trapped in a pointless debate around openness and closedness, around perfect transmission and ideological blockages. This discourse has a very long history, to the Frankfurt School and beyond. And the inverse discourse, from within the twentieth-century avant-garde, is equally stuffy: debates around apparatus critique, the notion that one must make the apparatus visible, that the "author" must be a "producer," and so on. It is a Brechtian mode, a Godardian mode, a Benjaminian mode. The *Mad* image implicitly participates in this tradition, despite being lowbrow and satirical in tone. In other words, to the extent that the *Mad* image is foregrounding the apparatus, it is not dissimilar to the sorts of formal techniques seen in the new wave, in modernism, and in other corners of the twentieth-century avant-garde.

Speaking aloud, the *Mad* image says: "I admit that an edge to the image exists – even if in the end it's all a joke – since the edge is visible within the fabric of my own construction." But the Rockwell image says: "Edges and centers may be the subject of art, but they are never anything that will influence the technique of art."

The *intraface* is the word used to describe this imaginary dialogue between the workable and the unworkable: the intraface, that is, *an interface internal to the interface.* The intraface is within the aesthetic. It is not a window or doorway separating the space that spans from here to there. Gérard Genette, in his book *Thresholds*, calls it a " 'zone of indecision' between the inside and outside."[10] It is no longer a question of choice, as it was with Dagognet. It is now a question of nonchoice. The intraface is *indecisive* for it must always juggle two things (the edge and the center) at the same time.

What exactly is the zone of indecision? What two things face off in the intraface? It is a type of aesthetic that implicitly brings together the edge and the center. The intraface may thus be defined as an internal interface between the edge and the center but one that is now entirely subsumed and con-

Text	Paratext
Diegetic	Nondiegetic
Image	Frame
Studium	*Punctum*
Aristotle	Brecht
Rockwell	*Mad*
Hitchcock	Godard
Transparency	Foregrounding
Dromenon	Algorithm
Realism	Function
Window	Mirror
3D model	Heads-up-display
Half-Life	*World of Warcraft*
Representation	Metrics
Narcissus	Echo

Figure 1.3. Centers and Edges.

tained within the image. This is what constitutes the zone of indecision.

Only now the discussion gets slightly more complicated, for consider the following query: Where does political art happen? In many cases – and I refer now to the historically specific mode of political art-making that comes out of modernism – the right column (Fig. 1.3) is the place where politicized or avant-garde culture takes place. Consider, for example, the classic debate between Aristotle and Augusto Boal: Aristotle, in his text on poetics, describes a cohesive representational mode oriented around principles of fear, pity, psychological reversal, and emotional catharsis, while Boal addresses himself to breaking down existing conventions within the expressive mode in order that mankind's political instinct might awaken.

The edge of the work is thus an arrow pointing to the outside, that is, pointing to the actually existing social and historical reality in which the work sits. Genette's "indecision" is, in this light, a codeword for something else: *historical materialism.* The edges of the work are the politics of the work.

To understand the true meaning of these two columns (Fig. 1.3) we might consider an example drawn from contemporary play culture, *World of Warcraft.* What does one notice immediately about the image (Fig. 1.4)? First, where is the diegetic space? It is the banquet hall interior, the deep volumetric mode of representation that comes directly out of Renaissance perspective techniques in painting. Alternately, where is the nondiegetic space? It is the thin, two-dimensional overlay containing icons, text, progress bars, and numbers. It deploys an entirely different mode of signification, reliant more on letter and number, iconographic images rather than realistic representational images.

Here the interface is awash in information. Even someone unfamiliar with the game will notice that the nondiegetic portion of the interface is as important if not more so than the diegetic portion. Gauges and dials have superseded lenses and windows. Writing is once again on par with image. It represents a sea change in the composition of media. In essence, the same process is taking place in *World of Warcraft* that took place in the *Mad* magazine cover. The diegetic space of the image is demoted in value and ultimately determined by a very complex nondiegetic mode of signification. So *World of Warcraft* is another way to think about the tension inside the medium. It is no longer a question of a "window" interface between this side of the screen and that side (for which of course it must also perform double duty), but an intraface between the heads-up-display, the text and icons in the foreground, and the 3D, volumetric, diegetic space of the game itself – on the one side, writing; on the other, image.

Each part of the interface has its role to play. But what else flows from this? The existence of the internal interface within the medium is important because it indicates the implicit presence of the outside within the inside. And, again to be unambiguous, "outside" means something quite specific: *the social.*

Figure 1.4. Blizzard Entertainment. *World of Warcraft*, 2004. Game still.

Each of the terms previously held in opposition – nondiegetic/ diegetic, paratext/text, the alienation effects of Brecht/emotional catharsis of Aristotle – each of these essentially refers to the tension between a progressive aesthetic movement (again, largely associated with but not limited to the twentieth century) and a more conventional one.

Now the examination of *World of Warcraft* can reach its full potential. For the question is never simply a formal claim, that this or that formal detail (text, icon, the heads-up-display) exists and may or may not be significant. No, the issue is a much greater one. If the nondiegetic takes center stage, we can be sure that the "outside," or the social, has been woven more intimately into the very fabric of the aesthetic than in previous times. In short, *this game is Brechtian*, if not in its actually existing political values, then at least through the values spoken at the level of mediatic form. (The hemming and hawing over what this actually means for progressive movements today is a valid question, one that I leave for another time.) In other words, games like *World of Warcraft* allow us to perform a very specific type of social analysis because they are telling us a story about contemporary life. Of course, it is common for popular media formats to tell the story of their own times; yet the level of unvarnished testimony available in a game like *World of Warcraft* is stunning. It is not an avant-garde image, but, nevertheless, it firmly delivers an avant-garde lesson in politics. At root, the game is not simply a fantasy landscape of dragons and epic weapons but a factory floor, an information-age sweatshop, custom tailored in every detail for cooperative ludic labor.

Politics thus reveals why the door or window theory of the interface is inadequate. The door-window model, handed down from McLuhan, can only ever reveal one thing, that the interface is a palimpsest. It can only ever reveal that the interface is a reprocessing of some other media that came before.

On this point I will be absolutely clear: a palimpsest the interface may be; yet it is still more useful to take the ultimate step, to suggest that the layers of the palimpsest themselves are "data" that must be interpreted. To this end, it is more useful to analyze the intraface using the principle of parallel aesthetic events, and to claim that these parallel events reveal something about the medium and about contemporary life. As I've already suggested, the proper label for this is allegory. And on this note it is now appropriate to revisit the "grand choice" mentioned in the opening section on methodology: that representation is either beautiful or deceptive; either intuitive or interpretable. A third way was never mentioned, not Iris or Hermes but the "kindly ones," the Eumenides also known as the Furies. For representation, as in Aeschylus' play, is an incontinent body, a frenzy of agitation issuing forth from the social body (the chorus). An elemental methodological relation thus exists between my three central themes: (1) the structure of allegory today, (2) the intraface, and (3) the dialectic between culture and history.

Regimes of Signification

Leaving this discussion of *World of Warcraft*, albeit brief, we are now able to return to Norman Rockwell and *Mad* magazine and, extrapolating from these two modes, make an initial claim about how certain types of digital media deal with the socio-technical interface. The alert observer might argue: "But doesn't the Rockwell image confess its own intimate knowledge of looking and mirroring, of frames and centers, just as astutely as the *Mad* image, only minus the juvenile one-liner? If so, wouldn't this make for a more sophisticated image? Why denigrate the image for being well made?" And this is true. The Rockwell image is indeed well crafted and exhibits a highly sophisticated understanding of how interfaces work. My claim is less a normative evaluation elevating one mode over the other and more an observation about how flows of signification organize a certain knowledge of the world and a commitment to it.

I will therefore offer a formula of belief and enactment: *Rockwell believes in the interface but doesn't enact it, while* Mad *enacts the interface, but doesn't believe in it.*

The first believes in the interface because it attempts to put the viewer, as a subject, into an imaginative space where interfaces propagate and transpire in full view and without anxiety. But at the same time, as media, as an illustration with its own borders, it does not enact the logic of the interface, for it makes it invisible. Hence it believes in it but doesn't enact it.

In contrast, the second voyages to a weird beyond filled with agitation and indecision and, in arriving there, turns the whole hoary system into a silly joke. Hence it enacts it but doesn't believe in it. If the first is a deobjectification of the interface, the second is an objectification of it. The first aims to remove all material traces of the medium, propping up the wild notion that the necessary trauma of all thresholds might be sublimated into mere "content," while the second objectifies the trauma itself into a "process-object" in which the upheaval of social forms are maintained in their feral state, but only within the safe confines of comic disbelief.

Coherence and incoherence have already been mentioned, and I would now like to make some more general observations about these concepts and their relationship to the interface. First, to revisit the terminology: coherence and incoherence compose a sort of continuum, which one might contextualize within the twin domains of the aesthetic and the political. These are as follows:

(1) Starting with the "coherent aesthetic," one might observe, simply, that it works. The gravity of the coherent aesthetic tends toward the center of the work of art. It is a process of centering, of gradual coalescing around a specific being. Examples of this may be found broadly across many media. Barthes' concept of the *studium* is its basic technique.

(2) An "incoherent aesthetic," by contrast, is one that doesn't work. Here gravity is not a unifying force but a force of degradation, tending to unravel neat masses into their unkempt, incontinent elements. "Incoherent" must not be understood with any normatively negative connotation: the point is not that the aesthetic is somehow unwatchable, or unrepresentable. Coherence and incoherence refer instead to the capacity of forces within the object, and whether they tend to coalesce or disseminate. Thus the *punctum*, not the *studium*, is the correct heuristic for this second mode.

(3) Replacing the aesthetic with the political, a "coherent politics" refers to the tendency to organize around a central formation. This brand of politics produces stable institutions, ones that involve centers of operation, known fields and capacities for regulating the flow of bodies and languages. This has been called a process of "state" formation or a "territorialization." Coherent politics include highly precise languages for the articulation of social beings. Evidence of their existence may be seen across a variety of actually existing political systems including fascism and national socialism but also liberal democracy.

(4) Ending with the fourth combination, an "incoherent politics" is one that tends to dissolve existing institutional bonds. It does not gravitate toward a center nor does it aspire to bring together existing formations into movements or coalitions. It comes under the name of "deterritorialization," of the event, of what some authors optimistically term "radical democracy." The principle here is not that of repeating past performance, of gradually resisting capitalism, or what have you, as in the example of Marx's mole. Instead, one must follow a break with the present, not simply by realizing one's desires, but by renovating the very meaning of desire itself.

(To reiterate, coherent and incoherent are nonnormative terms; they must be understood more as "aligned or unaligned" or "fixed or not fixed" rather than "good or bad" or "desirable or undesirable." I have already hinted at the analogous terms used by Deleuze, "territorialization" and "deterritorialization," but different authors use different terminology. For example, in Heidegger, the closest cognates are "falling" [*verfallen*] and "thrownness" [*Geworfenheit*].)

Here arrayed, the four modes may be paired up in various combinations, arriving at a number of different regimes of signification. First, the pairing of a coherent aesthetic with a coherent politics is what is typically known as *ideology* – the more sympathetic term is "myth," the less sympathetic is "propaganda." Thus in the ideological regime, a certain homology is achieved between the fixity of the aesthetic and the fixity of the political desire contained therein. (This is *not* to say that for any ideological formation there exists a specific, natural association between the aesthetic and the political but simply that there is a similarity by virtue of their both being coherent.) Hence any number of ideological and propagandistic cultural forms, from melodrama to Michael Moore, Matthew Arnold but also Marx, would be included in this regime. Given the references evoked earlier, it would be appropriate to associate Rockwell with this regime also, in that his image displays an aesthetic of coherence (the intense craft of illustration, the artist as genius, the swirling complexity of the creative process), and a politics of coherence (mom-and-apple-pie and only mom-and-apple-pie).

Edit the arrangements and a second pairing becomes visible. Connect an aesthetic of incoherence with a politics of coherence, and one arrives at the *ethical* regime of signification.[11] Here there is always a "fixed" political aspiration that comes into being through the application of various self-revealing or self-annihilating techniques within the aesthetic apparatus. For example, in the typical story of progressive twentieth-century culture, the one told in Alain Badiou's *The Century* for example, the ethical regime revolves around various flavors of modernist-inspired leftist progressivism. Thus, in Brecht, there is an aesthetic of incoherence (alienation effect, fore-grounding the apparatus), mated with a politics of coherence (Marx and only Marx). Or again, to evoke the central reference from above, the *Mad* image offers an aesthetic of incoherence (break the fourth wall, embrace optical illusion), combined with a politics of coherence (lowbrow and only lowbrow). And of course, many more names could be piled on: Jean-Luc Godard in film (tear film apart to shore up Marxist-Leninism); Fugazi in punk (tear sound apart in the service of the D.I.Y. lifestyle); and so on. However, it should be pointed out that modernist-inspired leftist progressivism is not the end of the story for the ethical regime. I intimated already, by calling the game Brechtian, that I wish to classify *World of Warcraft* under this regime. (And likewise, in the introduction to the book, I have already called computers "ethical" *in toto*.) But why? The reasons have already been given: the game displays an aesthetic of incoherence in that it foregrounds the apparatus (statistical data, machinic functions, respawn loops, object interfaces, multithreading, and so on), while all the time promoting a particularly coherent politics (protocological organization, networked integration, alienation from the traditional social order, new informatic labor practices, computer-mediated group interaction, neoliberal markets, game theory, and so forth). So, *World of Warcraft* is an "ethical" game simply by virtue of the way in which it opens up the aesthetic on the one hand while closing down politics on the other. Again, I am using a general (not a moral) definition of the term ethical, as a set of broad principles for practice within some normative framework. That *World of Warcraft* has more to do with the information economy, and Godard's *La Chinoise* has more to do with Maoism, does not diminish either in its role within the ethical regime.

Mode three appears now, a mode which may be labeled *poetic* in that it combines an aesthetic of coherence with a politics of incoherence. This regime is seen often in certain brands of modernism, particularly the highly formal, inward-looking wing known as "art for art's sake" but also, more generally, in all manner of fine art. It is labeled "poetic" simply because it aligns itself with *poesis*, or meaning-making in a general sense. The stakes are not those of metaphysics, in which any image is measured against its original, but rather the semiautonomous "physics" of art, that is, the tricks and techniques that contribute to success or failure within mimetic representation as such. Aristotle was the first to document these tricks and techniques, in his *Poetics*, and the general personality of the poetic regime as a whole has changed little since. In this regime, lie the great geniuses of their craft (for this is the regime within which the concept of "genius" finds its natural home): Alfred Hitchcock or Billy Wilder, Deleuze or Heidegger, much of modernism, all of minimalism, and so on. But you counter: "Certainly the work of Heidegger or Deleuze was political. Why classify them here?" The answer lies in the specific nature of politics in the two thinkers and the way in which the art of philosophy is elevated over other concerns. My claim is not that these various figures are not political but simply that their politics is "unaligned" and therefore *incoherent*. Eyal Weizman has written of the way in which the Israeli Defense Forces have deployed the teachings of Deleuze and Félix Guattari in the field of battle. This speaks not to a corruption of the thought of Deleuze and Guattari but to the very receptivity of the work to a variety of political implementations (that is, to its "incoherence"). To take Deleuze and Guattari to Gaza is not to blaspheme them but to deploy them. Michael Hardt and Negri, and others have shown also how the rhizome has been adopted as a structuring diagram for systems of hegemonic power. Again this is not to malign Deleuze and Guattari but simply to point out that their work is politically "open source." The very inability to align a specific political content of these thinkers is evidence that it is fundamentally poetic (and not ethical). In other words, the "poetic" regime is always receptive to diverse political adaptations, for it leaves the political question open. This is perhaps another way to approach the concept of a "poetic ontology," the label Badiou gives to both Deleuze and Heidegger. And while Badiou's thought is no less poetic, with its song to the great redeemers, Art, Love, Politics, and Science, he ultimately departs from the "poetic" regime thanks to an intricate – and militantly specific – political theory.

Under-appreciated and elusive, the final mode has never achieved any sort of bona fide existence in modern culture, neither in the dominant position nor in the various "tolerated" subaltern positions. This is the dirty regime wherein aesthetic incoherence interfaces with political incoherence. We shall call it simply *truth*, although other terms might also suffice (nihilism, radical alterity, the inhuman). The truth regime always remains on the sidelines. It appears not through a "return of the repressed," for it is never merely the dominant's repressed other. Instead, it might best be understood as "the repressed of the repressed," or using terminology from another time and another place, "the negation of the negation." May we associate certain names with this mode, with an incoherence in both aesthetics and politics? May we associate the names of Nietzsche? Of Georges Bataille? Of Jacques Derrida? The way forward is not so certain. But it is perhaps better left that way for the time being.

Listing them together, here are the four regimes of signification:

(1) Ideological: an aesthetic of coherence, a politics of coherence;
(2) Ethical: an aesthetic of incoherence, a politics of coherence;
(3) Poetic: an aesthetic of coherence, a politics of incoherence;
(4) Truth: an aesthetic of incoherence, a politics of incoherence.

This system requires some commentary before closing. First, the entire classification system seems to say something about the relationship between art and justice. In the first regime, art and justice are coterminous. One need only internalize the one to arrive at the other. In the second, the process is slightly different: one must destroy art in the service of justice. In the third it is inverted: one must banish the category of justice entirely to witness the apotheosis of art. And finally, in the fourth, redemption comes in the equal destruction of all existing standards of art and all received models of justice. Second, after closer examination of these four regimes, it is clear that a hierarchy exists, if not for all time, then at least for the specific cultural and historical formation in which we live. That is to say: the first mode is dominant (albeit often maligned), the second is privileged, the third is tolerated, and the final is relatively sidelined.

I have thus presented them here in order of priority. But the hierarchy has little value unless it can be historicized. Thus an additional claim is helpful, reiterated from the above section on *World of Warcraft*: if anything can be said about the changing uses of these regimes in the age of ludic economies it would be that we are witnessing today a general shift in primacy from the first to the second, that is to say, from the "ideological" regime to the "ethical" regime. As we will explore next in Chapter 2, ideology is in recession today, at least in terms of its classical effectivity; there is a decline in ideological efficiency. Ideology, which was traditionally defined as an "imaginary relationship to real conditions" (Althusser), has in some senses succeeded too well and, as it were, put itself out of a job. Instead, we have simulation, which must be understood as something like an "imaginary relationship to ideological conditions." In short, ideology gets *modeled* in software. So in the very perfection of the ideological regime, in the form of its pure digital simulation, comes the death of the ideological regime, and simulation is "crowned winner" as the absolute horizon of the ideological world. The computer is the ultimate ethical machine. It has no actual relation with ideology in any proper sense of the term, only a virtual relation.

Passing from the ideological regime to the ethical regime does *not* mean that today's climate is any more or less "ethical" (in the sense of good deed doing) or more or less politicized than the past. Remember that the ethical mode (#2) is labeled "ethical" because it adopts various normative techniques wherein given aesthetic dominants are shattered (via foregrounding the apparatus, alienation effects, and so on) in the service of a specific desired ethos.

Last, given that it is common to bracket both the ideological form (#1) and the truth form (#4), the one banished from respectable discourse out of scorn and the other out of fear, the system may be greatly simplified into just two regimes (#2 and #3), revealing a sort of primordial axiom: *the more coherent a work is aesthetically, the more incoherent it tends to be politically.* And the reverse is also true: *the more incoherent a work is aesthetically, the more coherent it tends to be politically.* The primordial axiom (of course it is no such thing, merely a set of tendencies arising from an analysis of actually existing cultural production) thus posits two typical cases, the ethical and the poetic. In simple language, the first is what we call politically significant art; the second is what we call fine art. The first is Godard, the second is Hitchcock. Or, if you like, the first is *World of Warcraft* and the second is *Half-Life*. The first enacts the mediatic condition but doesn't believe in it; the second believes in the mediatic condition but doesn't enact it.

Ending in this way, we might return to our mantra, that the interface is a medium that does not mediate. It is unworkable. The difficulty, however, lies not in this dilemma but in the fact that the interface never admits it. It is true that it is false. It describes itself as a door or a window or some other sort of threshold across which we must simply step to receive the bounty beyond. But a thing and its opposite are never joined by the interface in such a neat and tidy manner. This is not to say that incoherence wins out in the end, invalidating the other modes. Simply that there will be an intraface within the object between the aesthetic form of the piece and the larger historical material context in which it is situated. If an "interface" may be found anywhere, it is there. What are called "writing," or "image," or "object," are merely the attempts to resolve this unworkability.

2   Software and Ideology

Provides classes and interfaces for obtaining reflective information about classes and objects.

Description of the Java programming package
"java.lang.reflect," Sun Microsystems (2004).

An Analog . . .

In the previous chapter I described the interface as a general
mode of mediation. While readily evident in things like screens
and surfaces, the interface is ultimately something beyond
the screen. It has only a superficial relationship to the surfaces
of digital devices, those skins that beg to be touched. Rather,
the interface is a general technique of mediation evident at
all levels; indeed it facilitates the way of thinking that tends
to pitch things in terms of "levels" or "layers" in the first
place. These levels, these many interfaces, are the subject of
analysis not so much to explain what they are, but to show
that the social field itself constitutes a grand interface, an
interface between subject and world, between surface and
source, and between critique and the objects of criticism.
Hence the interface is above all an allegorical device that
will help us gain some perspective on culture in the age of
information. For this reason, we look now to the "deeper"
realm of software, the realm below the screen, with an eye to
the possible ideological construction of this hidden electronic
kingdom.

New media, and the software that drive it, has always had an interesting relationship with ideology. Some see new media as a liberating sword, cutting through the ideological fog of the old world, while others see new media as another apparatus of control, insinuating itself into every corner of our lives. For this reason I want to structure the present chapter around a particular essay, Wendy Hui Kyong Chun's fascinating "On Software, or the Persistence of Visual Knowledge," in which the claim is made, among other things, that "software is a functional analog to ideology."[1] The two moments contained in this claim – "an analog" "that is functional" – will help to structure the chapter. As brief as it is, Chun's claim nevertheless brings out a rich set of discussions, not least of which are the theory and history of both software and ideology, the question of *functionality*, and also the way in which something might be an analog for something else. Further, this last matter, the analog, is particularly apropos for an exploration of the process of interpretation and how cultural objects deploy modes of figuration such as allegory (an issue to which I will return at the end of the chapter). While the question of functionality will occupy the second half of this chapter it is worth defining now: I adopt the usage from computer science where a function is any subroutine or isolated block of code, but further from mathematics where a function is any expressive entity able to translate a set of inputs into a set of outputs. One of the first claims extracted from Chun is that there is a similarity, which we may call a formal similarity, between the structure of ideology and the structure of software. Conveniently, the desire to make such a claim can be folded into the quality of software itself: it is a technology of simulation and thus has as a core asset the ability to "take shape" in various ways. In other words, software is by definition formal (as symbolic or abstract mathematical and logical code), and thus it acclimates well to structural comparisons – even better than, one might argue, its cousins the visual image or verbal narrative. The analogical or "expressive" theory of ideology is also not unfamiliar, as in the work of Louis Althusser where the structure of ideology resembles, more or less, an architectural drawing of a house, with the material base of society down below and the cultural or superstructural layer up above. Ideology emerges not strictly as the house itself, but as a figurative projection of one layer onto the other. It is thus a stand in for what the Marxists simply call *history*, or in crass terms the ongoing reification of social relations and processes, and further the problem of being able to represent these details from the past in the present. If software is less a vehicle for ideology and more its simulation or model, it is no doubt because of these formal qualities of software which, combined with software's importance as so many cultural and historical artifacts, are so well suited for precise mathematical modeling of real world phenomena – in functionality, in spatial projection, in sight and sound – but in a manner in which the very material distance or empirical falsity of that simulation is at once foregrounded as a fatal flaw and then resolved as insignificant. "Ideology" is one name that may be used for things that act this way.

Gaps abound in such systems. And across these many gaps an intense mimetic thicket emerges: ideology as projection across the gap between individuals and their real conditions of existence; software as mimetic technology bridging the gap between machines and their logical simulation; and the startling claim, from Chun, that software could conceivably be a continuously variable copy (i.e. an analog) of ideology.

It would be logical to begin such a discussion by revisiting the classical theories of ideology, which I will do quickly now, ignoring for a moment that ideology and its own conceptualization in theoretical discourse seem to be at odds, for the power of ideology, if it has any at all, is the high level of constraint it puts on discourse itself, aiming for a system of total or "smooth" thought. Ideology is always about two things at the same time. First, ideology is a matter of life and culture, a representation of one's lived social relation (following Althusser's definition). But second, ideology is also implicitly a matter of *critique*, for as Jameson said once about capitalism, simply to utter the word "ideology" seems to indicate one's disdain for it. In discourse on the subject, a first motif, that of *scientific thought*, suggests that ideology is always set up in distinction to other styles of thinking. Yet the history of the concept takes a detour here, for whereas Destutt de Tracy, who coined the term in the 1790s, championed his new science of ideology as an antidote to philosophy and metaphysics (and later was famously lambasted by Napoleon for caring little about the "knowledge of the human heart" and "the lessons of history"), Althusser, by contrast, reverses the sophistry narrative, positing Marxist critique as scientific and ideology as the threat to clear thinking.

Running a close second to the scientific narrative is the *narrative of political failure*. Here, ideology serves as a sort of anthropological "explanation" for all sorts of alienation, exploitation, and false consciousness existing in society, along the lines of the doctrine of original sin or the great theological arguments for the existence of evil as explanation for why the here and now is so inferior to the hereafter. This is an essentially strategic theory of ideology, evident in Gramsci and others, that serves as theoretical proof for the nonexistence of the revolution, despite the perception that all the necessary real world phenomenon are in place for it to arrive at any moment. (This same political messianism is addressed quite compellingly in Derrida's *The Specters of Marx*).

Ultimately these first two narratives are synthesized into a third, ideology's *determinism narrative* in which ideology is understood as a system of total thought that may or may not determine things like human subjects. Here we may include the work of the Frankfurt School, or again Althusser, with the key issue being the industrialization of the body and mind into ever more insidious modes of efficiency and instrumentality. Likewise we might return here to Marx and Engels, particularly the so-called "dominant ideology thesis" extracted from passages in the *Communist Manifesto* as well as certain references to the determination of consciousness in *The German Ideology*.

Marx's theory of ideology, such as it is, has long been critiqued for its determinism. But the theory of ideology was recuperated in the later part of the twentieth century by what might be thought of as the *synthetic narrative*: ideology is not a one-way street, but is always meted out at the intersection of cultural production and cultural consumption. In this context, ideology follows a more dialectical logic, as with Jameson's two terms "reification and utopia" (a formulation from *Signatures of the Visible*, the terms of which shift slightly to the "utopia and ideology" of *The Political Unconscious*), or with Stuart Hall's well-known theory of "articulation," or indeed earlier with Gramsci's notion of hegemony in which political or cultural dominance is always the result of active negotiation and production.

Ideology is not something that can be solved like a puzzle, or cured like a disease. Even with all these various and sometimes conflicting themes from the many theories of ideology, it would be shortsighted to write off the concept as some sort of cognitive delusion, a fog of false consciousness afflicting the minds of those it touches. Instead ideology is better understood as a problematic, that is to say a conceptual interface in which theoretical problems arise and are generated and sustained precisely as problems in themselves. Following Chun's lead, it appears that software too must be understood not as a given social and technical object, but as a problematic interface – indeed, one that is continuously in the process of producing its own status as social and technical. (In this sense "problem" is a synonym for "interface," which is itself a stand-in candidate for "software.")

Most discussions of software require a significant amount of back-peddling at the outset, owing to a number of confusions and difficulties with the concept. The first difficulty is that software, in different ways and in different amounts, customarily stands in opposition to the notion of the qualitative or the continuous, often summed up as the "realm of the analog." (Although the term analog is so often misused it should be uttered with extreme care.) While this analog-digital polarity is thorny in itself, we must be particularly attentive given the current discussion, as the topic of the analogical has already been broached in Chun's description of the internal modeling of software as something like ideology-in-code. Second, software relies on the assumption that there is something like a programmer and something like a user. This also presents a special set of problems, the most important of which is the status of the actor versus the acted-upon (the aforementioned determinism narrative), and under what circumstances which is which. Today the "culture industry" takes on a whole new meaning, for inside software the "cultural" and the "industrial" are coterminous (which is why it is tautological to speak today of a cultural logic of informatics). The detailed forms of algorithmic interaction and play required today of the computer-using public is, in my mind, so exactly akin to writing code that the division between the two must certainly be ascribed to other ends. Perhaps it has to do with the creation and maintenance of another class of priest-like specialists striving to decode software just as the critic longs to "reverse engineer" ideology, or perhaps it is best to contextualize it within the long standing debates around groups of producers and groups of consumers, and the implicit power dynamics haunting their mutual distinction. A third difficulty is the notion that, in using the concept of software, one is somehow excluding hardware. This flows from a long-standing assumption that data is fundamentally immaterial or ethereal and that, conversely, machines are the stuff of material cogs and levers. It is a foundational claim stemming from the very first informatic machines. But as Chun and others have pointed out, "programming" a computer originally meant patching circuits together using cables or connectors and thus "software" began historically not as executable software applications as we know them today but as any sort of service labor performed in or on informatic machines; even video was once known as "software," to distinguish it from "hard" playback decks and cameras. Thus the interface effect is also a kind of segregation effect whereby data is relegated to the realm of ideas and machines to the realm of technology. This results in a presentism, admittedly parroted by me here, where software is understood only in its late-twentieth-century definition as a symbolic machine language and not in an earlier definition in which software might rightly be understood as pre- or non-linguistic.

Unraveling such logic is challenging. Friedrich Kittler tried to tackle it in his essay "There is No Software," which I already referenced briefly in the introduction. The essay is a clever if sometimes casual unpacking of the strict division placed between code and machines. The conceit of the essay's title is that, indeed, software is merely a human-friendly category extracted from what is always an operation of hardware. Logic gates are electronic machines; they are physical devices through and through. Voltages in electronic circuits are material, not immaterial (whatever that may be). As it was in Parmenides: what is not, cannot be. So one must assume that the "soft" comes from the informatic fluidity of these devices, from what Turing meant when he called his machine "universal" rather than "discrete." When basic logic gate functionality is abstracted and strung together into machine commands, translated into assembly op-codes, and then later articulated in a higher level computer language such as C, the argument from Kittler is that one should never understand this "higher" symbolic machine as anything empirically different from the "lower" symbolic interactions of voltages through logic gates. They are complex aggregates yes, but it is foolish to think that writing an "if-then" control structure in eight lines of assembly code is any more or less machinic than doing it in one line of C, just as the same quadratic equation may swell with any number of multipliers and still remain balanced. The relationship between the two is *technical*.

Still its being technical does not excuse it from being *interesting*, particularly on the question of ideology. It simply requires that we speak in terms of a machine aesthetics, rather than a verbal or visual aesthetics. What I shall propose here is that *software is an example of technical transcoding, without figuration, that nevertheless coexists with an exceedingly high level of ideological fetishism and misrecognition*. (Is this not, after all, the very definition of technology?) Chun makes this connection explicitly: "Software is based on a fetishistic logic. Users know very well that their folders and desktops are not really folders and desktops, but they treat them as if they were – by referring to them as folders and desktops."[2] Whether this is truly a fetishistic logic, or an allegory for one, remains to be determined. In Marx, fetishism comes from the expressive and figurative logic of representation – how value appears in the form of something that it isn't – a fact no doubt that allowed a Marxist methodology to translate easily to other intellectual fields also dealing with the problem of representation (semiotics, art history, literary criticism, theories of race, and so on). But of course the strength of Marx's analysis in *Capital* is that he derived fetishism from a fundamentally empirical, or "technical," set of relations (the rule of market exchange, the standardization of labor power, the sciences of productivity and efficiency, the operation of machines, and so on). Thus a dialectic of technical transcoding and fetishistic abstraction exists from the start. This is why I will suggest at the end of the chapter that the relationship between software and ideology is best understood as an allegorical one: software is not merely a vehicle for ideology; instead, the ideological contradictions of technical transcoding and fetishistic abstraction are enacted and "resolved" within the very form of software itself.

New media hide as much as they show, and the ultimate power of Chun's essay is found in a symptom, an idea that appears in the title but then hides itself during most of her essay just as fiercely as it proclaims itself at the start. For Chun the interface between software and ideology is a throwback: it is *visual* knowledge that persists inside software. Thus one might assume that the visual quality of knowledge is the key to the software/ideology puzzle. "The computer," she writes, "that most nonvisual and nontransparent device – has paradoxically fostered 'visual culture' and 'transparency.' "[3] Software purists will doubtless be put off by this, as will those more familiar with the intellectual terrain of visual culture, to which the topics of my writings, admittedly, are only related through a sort of counterintuitive leap. If I may read between the lines of Chun's essay, it is not exactly the discipline of visual culture that provides a backdrop for her project, despite the use of the term "visual" and despite indications made in her book *Control and Freedom*. And here things start to get thorny, for one must make a distinction between the "visible," which is typically understood as specific to the faculty of optical sight, and the "visual," which might be understood in broader, more figurative strokes as an epistemic process of cognitive understanding and conceptualization: one may speak of mental "insight" with or without the optical faculty, just as one might "see" an image inside of a dream. This results in the sorts of claims, astounding at first blush, made by W.J.T. Mitchell most recently in *What Do Pictures Want?* that the core, genetic formation of culture is not the text or even the idea, but the *image.*

Of course, to read Mitchell (or Chun) sympathetically would not be to assume he believes that the world is made up exclusively of semiotic interfaces like television screens, advertisements, paintings, film reels, and corporate logos – no, these are not the "images" he means, at least not only. Instead, the "visual" might better be understood as referring to any likeness or motif that fixes some grouping of elements, such that one might "see" these elements both as a relational whole (as a memory, refrain, gesture, raster, etc.) and also in terms of their constituent parts (phoneme, texture, color, pitch, pixel). This is not such a dramatic claim, however, and it is certainly one that runs parallel with Western philosophy and aesthetics from the get go. Thus, the enlightenment episteme, which unites (some might say collapses) knowledge and the visual in various technologies of representational transparency and communicability, persists in software, argues Chun, not only because of the conceptualizations and "sightings" just mentioned, but also to the extent that it promotes a depth model of representation between sources and surfaces, scripts and screens, the code and the user. But the enlightenment model has also provoked a whole flock of criticism, rightly, around the impossibility of such transparent representation. Thus we arrive at a paradox: any mediating technology is obliged to erase itself to the highest degree possible in the name of unfettered communication, but in so doing it proves its own virtuosic presence as technology thereby undoing the original erasure. "What is software," Chun writes, "if not the very effort of making something explicit, or making something intangible visible, while at the same time rendering the visible (such as the machine) invisible?"[4] Language wants to be overlooked. But it wants to be overlooked precisely so that it can more effectively "over look," that is, so that it can better function as a syntactic and semantic system designed to specify and articulate while remaining detached from the very processes of specificity and articulation. This is one sense in which language, which itself is not necessarily connected to optical sight, can nevertheless be "visual."

Chun's suggestion is that to understand software we must return to a discussion of the visual and the ideology problems contained therein, not skip forward to some purely machinic, and hence chiefly nonvisual, aesthetic realm. This is good advice, but the appeal to visual knowledge must still be understood in a figurative, not literal (i.e. optical), sense, for as I will argue below it is more valuable to separate rather than collapse software's visual and machinic aspects in mutually distinct struggle, for this separation simulates the same struggle writ large in the socio-political arena between an informatic or machinic model of organization and a slightly older one which takes as its prized aesthetic forms of the verbal narrative and the visible image. In other words, the separation between the visual and the machinic in software is important because it is an allegory of the social. Chun's "persistence of visual knowledge" signifies the double bind of what some optimistically call the information age: it underscores the fact that software is rooted in symbolic logic not optical vision, and thus cannot fully leverage the dominant form existing even now in the spectacle society, yet at the same time gains inroads precisely at the expense of that social form that it so effectively simulates.

The history of visuality and computing is a complicated history. It is certainly incorrect to divorce one from the other, as authors like Lev Manovich have rightly pointed out (see in particular his essay "The Automation of Sight"). Indeed any understanding of contemporary visual mediation that ignores software does so at its own peril, in an age when cinema has become synonymous with Final Cut Pro, photography with Photoshop, writing with Microsoft Word, and on and on. The history of the pixel is instructive in this capacity: at its invention in the middle twentieth century the electronic pixel was essentially the same thing as the binary bit, one existing in the modality of visible light and the other existing in the modality of mathematical value. But at the same time I am sympathetic to a certain minoritarian refrain running through recent media theory on the specificity of computers as non-optical if not altogether non-visual media, for anyone wishing to cram computers into the framework of "visual culture" is certainly suffering from an unfortunate fetishization of the physical interface, as if the computer monitor were an adequate substitute for the medium as a whole, which, in addition to screens of various shapes and sizes, consists of any number of other technologies: nonoptical interfaces (keyboard, mouse, controller, sensor); data in memory and data on disk; executable algorithms; networking technologies and protocols; and the list continues. The fields of computer vision and computer graphics are also but a fraction of computer science as a whole which occupies most all of its time with algorithms, data structures, cryptography, robotics, bioinformatics, networking, machine learning, and other nonvisual applications of symbolic systems.[5]

Each of these domains deserves a deeper level of attention. But while leaving this discussion of the visual somewhat unresolved, I return to the overarching theme, the interface, by offering the first of two general observations on software and ideology. Software operates through a technological model that places a great premium on meticulous symbolic declarations and descriptions, yet at the same time requires concealment, encapsulation, and obfuscation of large portions of code. This is why programmers talk in terms of "software interfaces" or "application interfaces." Formulated as an assertion, *software requires both reflection and obfuscation.* If software is indeed an allegorical analog to ideology, it should come as no surprise that software functions in such a dialectical fashion. The critics of ideology have often described it in synthetic terms (Jameson, Hall, Gramsci, et al.). But software has its own technologies of reflection and obfuscation. *Reflection* is nearly axiomatic: the complete syntactic and semantic rules of a computer language must be defined and written into any environment designed to interpret, parse, or execute it. (As an aside: in the so-called natural languages this is never the case, despite style guides and dictionaries, as unforeseen "inductive" uses of language may be stumbled upon or invented without the blessing of provenance, whereas with software the unforeseen articulations of language are essentially dismissed out of hand as errors or "exceptions." Of course, this does not foreclose on the possibility, nay necessity, for hacks and other software exploits to pop up in the complexity of the software network, exploits which can never be predicted, as the computer scientists would say, "statically." The difference is that exploits operate *intensively* within and through the rules of the symbolic system, while natural languages operate extensively as a result of a combinatorial discursive logic ever intent on probing the boundaries of allowable style.) Reflective sandboxing of software code within a machine built to parse it is seen in the case of a computer language like Java which must be compiled and then run as bytecode inside a special runtime environment, or, as with the language C, compiled and then run as "native" machine instructions, or with a simple mark up language like HTML the specifications for which must be entirely designed into any browser destined to interpret and display it, or also with other interpreted code such as a three-dimensional model whose mathematical values for vertices and textures must be transcoded according to the rules of a given data format and a given style of visual projection. This existential, or meta-medial reflection is further illustrated in the "system" or "global" paratextual variables existent in many languages. Perl's implementation is particularly dazzling: $$ for the process number, $! for the last system call error, and $0 for the program name; Java too, which includes special "meta" objects such as the package java.lang.reflect and the class java.lang.Class that are designed to obtain information about classes and objects.[6] These meta objects are used to write reflexive software such as debuggers or interpreters, or to declare new objects dynamically during runtime. Indeed ontology itself, formerly a branch of philosophy, is now also a branch of computer science appearing perhaps most visibly in Web ontology standards such as OWL (Web Ontology Language).

Encapsulation and *transcoding* are two useful ways for understanding the technology of obfuscation. The principle of transcoding, which I am adopting from Manovich, states that new media objects may be converted digitally from one data structure to another, but further that there are entire media formats based entirely on such conversions and nothing more. Thus an application like BIND (Berkeley Internet Name Domain), a leading domain name resolver, exists so that IP addresses can be masked by more human-legible domain names. The netmask is similar: in binary math, a bit within a binary number can be extracted using a special masking number and an "and" bitwise operation; likewise in network addressing, subnets are defined using a special number called a netmask that specifies a section of the network address for the subnet itself and then "masks" or obfuscates the rest to be used by the hosts residing on the subnet. In a bitmap image numerical values are used to represent color intensities in a pixel grid. Yet they are never represented as such, but instead are converted into data signals and sent to the display adapter which then converts these values into voltages that appear as light on a screen (the aforementioned modal transformation from bit to pixel). So in this case "conversion" is a certain conjunction between "physical" signal and "abstract" number where one is hidden at the expense of the other. Even the HTML example referenced previously uses the same principle of data hiding: HTML is never shown in the browser window, it is always parsed and converted from ASCII text into a graphical layout (which may or may not also include ASCII text).

These are only a few examples of the larger trend in software design to hide numerical encoding of data behind more privileged "semantic" formats such as natural language or graphics. In this way, *numbers essentially follow an occult logic*: they are hidden at exactly the moment when they express themselves. Chun calls this "the nonreflection of changeable facts in software."[7] In fact encapsulation is rather dominant in the area of code authorship and compilation. The most fundamental design principle for object-oriented computer languages is the combination of variables and operations on variables (methods) into something called a class. Classes can be instantiated as objects and these objects interact through the ability to send messages to other objects via object interfaces. This is where encapsulation comes in: the details of how an object implements any given operation are deliberately kept hidden from any other object making requests of it. For example, a method's input and output might be visible but how it processes the input into the output is kept hidden. In order to implement the technologies of encapsulation, a system of visibility modifiers are employed, as in the case of Java whereby classes, methods, or variables may be deemed "public," "private," or "protected," each designation helping to determine if the class, method, or variable is visible to the rest of the code.

Code obfuscation, or "information hiding," is employed in order to make code more modular and abstract and thus easier to maintain. A class' method can be updated and, as long as it continues to fit its public interface "signature," one may be reasonably assured the code will continue to run. The following text articulates the rationale for obfuscation from the perspective of computer science.

> A major challenge – perhaps *the* major challenge – in the construction of any large body of software is how to divide the effort among programmers in such a way that work can proceed on multiple fronts simultaneously. This modularization of efforts depends critically on the notion of *information hiding*, which makes objects and algorithms invisible, whenever possible, to portions of the system that do not need them. Properly modularized code reduces the "cognitive load" on the programmer by minimizing the amount of information required to understand any given portion of the system. In a well-designed program the interfaces between modules are as "narrow" (i.e., simple) as possible, and any design decision that is likely to change is hidden inside a single module. This latter point is crucial, since maintenance (bug fixes and enhancement) consumes many more programmer years than does initial construction for most commercial software.
>
> In addition to reducing cognitive load, information hiding has several more pedestrian benefits. First, it reduces the risk of name conflicts: with fewer visible names, there is less chance that a newly introduced name will be the same as one already in use. Second, it safeguards the integrity of data abstractions: any attempt to access objects outside of the subroutine(s) to which they belong will cause the compiler to issue an "undefined

symbol" error message. Third, it helps to compartmentalize run-time errors: if a variable takes on an unexpected value, we can generally be sure that the code that modified it is in the variable's scope.[8]

On this point it pays to be overly literal. It is worth spelling out the significant similarity between such a description of the labor process and that same description offered by Marx and his progeny in the ideology discussion. In both cases we have an "object" imbued with a complex interface for hiding things, be it the commodity object (or as Guy Debord mania-cally demonstrated, the commodity as image) and its ability to mask its own history of production and the social division of labor that generated it, or be it the Java object and its ability to cordon off various functionality into this or that site of inscription and execution, which is no doubt an abstraction or *mapping* of the actual division of labor globally in the dot-com firm producing it, where one part of the code might spring from a desk in Redmond and another part from a desk in Bangalore without anyone being the wiser. The structure of software facilitates this larger social reality. This is not to promote some sort of conspiracy theory for the new economy, simply to note the significant formal similarities between the structure of software as a media technology and the structure of ideology – with the commodity as a waypoint between the two. (Recall that for figures like Debord, Jean-Joseph Goux, or Roland Barthes the commodity and ideology are nearly synonymous.)

New media is often lauded for championing the virtue of openness. Yet I stress that "reflection" and "obfuscation" have nothing to do with the debate around open source versus proprietary software. They have nothing to do with "good" uses of code versus "bad" uses. Open source software follows the principle of source concealment, just as proprietary software does. Hence it is not the ability to view the source that is at question, but whether or not the source is put front and center as the medium itself. And in nearly all software systems it is *not*. (Perhaps special allowances would have to be paid for things like disassemblers, hex editors, and software development kits.) Such realities are not un-germane to the fields of poetics or hermeneutics which often must deal with models of expression wherein the kernel of the work is relegated to the place of the ineffable, as in the "suggestion" or articulable "silence" of Symbolism or the masochistic disavowal of the cinema which can never truly recreate its subject, action through time and space, only depict it happening.

Such is the fundamental contradiction: what you see is not what you get. Software is the medium that is not a medium. Information interfaces are always "unworkable." Code is never viewed as it is. Instead code must be compiled, interpreted, parsed, and otherwise driven into hiding by still larger globs of code. Hence the principle of *obfuscation*. But at the same time it is the exceedingly high degree of declarative reflexivity in software that allows it to operate so effectively as source or algorithmic essence – the stating of variables at the outset, the declarations of methods, all before the real "language" takes place – within a larger software environment always already predestined to parse and execute it. And hence the principle of *reflection*.

. . . That is Functional

Unworkable does not mean ineffectual. To describe a software interface as unworkable is not to describe it as inert or listless. So let us return to Chun's claim that "software is a functional analog to ideology." This indicates not only that software is an analog to ideology, but a much more fundamental claim, that software is *functional* in nature, therefore suggesting that ideology might be too. In other words, software is ideology turned machinic. I hinted at this above with reference to ideology's "determinism narrative." The discussion of the determinism narrative was meant to highlight the aspect of ideology that is oriented toward changing and inflecting the material world, the primary example of which would be the discussion of interpellation and subject formation in Althusser. In contrast, many have argued – Foucault famously – that it is really the reverse: ideology is not a prime mover that casts subjects in its image, but rather real social and technical apparatuses discipline and inflect the material resources immanent to them, be they human bodies or otherwise. The pattern of proscriptive constraints may not be new, but what is crucial in software is the translation of ideological force into data structures and symbolic logic, a process no doubt coterminous with the evolution of language itself. Software is algorithmically affective in ways that ideology never was. This is best understood not as evidence of a schism between software and ideology, but as the very consummation of the deterministic, expedient narratives of both.

Media are the expression of this functional mandate. But how does it work? The following slogan helps explain the functional nature of software: *code is the only language that is executable.* Speech act theory has dealt with such questions already for some time. Particularly relevant to the present discussion is the concept of an illocutionary speech act, defined as a verbal expression that when uttered changes some state of affairs in the world. Here is Katherine Hayles on the illocutionary quality of all code:

> Code has become arguably as important as natural language because it causes things to happen, which requires that it be executed as commands the machine can run.
>
> Code that runs on a machine is performative in a much stronger sense than that attributed to language. When language is said to be performative, the kinds of actions it "performs" happen in the minds of humans, as when someone says "I declare this legislative session open" or "I pronounce you husband and wife." Granted, these changes in minds can and do result in behavioral effects, but the performative force of language is nonetheless tied to the external changes through complex chains of mediation. By contrast, code running in a digital computer causes changes in machine behavior and, through networked ports and other interfaces, may initiate other changes, all implemented through transmission and execution of code.[9]

Illocutionary speech acts thus provide a basic structure for thinking about how code works. Yet not all agree on this point.

Opponents of the claim that all code is illocutionary point out that computer languages and natural languages are not different on the question of execution. They argue that illocutionary speech acts in natural languages require a general social understanding between groups of people in order for their performative quality to be effective – a pronouncement of marriage from the mouth of a priest creates a change in the world, but from an actor in a theater the same utterance exacts no such change – and likewise computer code requires a general infrastructure, the hardware of the computer, in order to carry out its "illocutionary" command. Yet I agree with Hayles: code is machinic first and linguistic second; an intersubjective infrastructure is not the same as a material one (even if making such a claim unfortunately splits these two symbolic systems into the "soft" natural languages versus the "hard" computer languages). To see code as subjectively performative or enunciative is to anthropomorphize it, to project it onto the rubric of psychology, rather than to understand it through its own logic of "calculation" or "command." The material substrate of code, which must always exist as an amalgam of electrical signals and logical operations in silicon, however large or small, demonstrates that code exists first and foremost as commands issued to a machine. Code essentially has no other reason for being than instructing some machine in how to act. One cannot say the same for the natural languages. (Elsewhere Chun complicates this line of reasoning with her evocative argument that source code is only ever understood as source code *after the fact*.) Of course this is not to exclude the cultural or technical importance of any code that runs *counter* to the perceived mandates of machinic execution, such as the computer glitch or the software exploit, simply to highlight the fundamentally functional nature of all software (glitch and exploit included).

Machines and narratives are not alike however. A tension remains between software, which I suggest is fundamentally a machine, and ideology, which is generally understood as a narrative of some sort or another. Espen Aarseth's heroic reworking of text and narrative into what he calls the "traversal functions" of electronic texts is indicative of how narrative cannot exist in code as such, but must be simulated, either as a "narrative" flow function governing specific semantic elements, or as an "image" of elements in relation as in the case of an array or a database. Software is not primarily a verbal narrative or a visual image, even if certainly these latter forms can be remediated in software. The problem stems from the two basic understandings of software, one as computer language and the other as machine. As language, software is a symbolic system that can exist in different modes, often understood as linguistic or code "layers" (the crux of Kittler's argument in "There is No Software"). As I argued above in the context of transcoding, one of the outcomes of this perspective is that each layer is technologically related, if not entirely equivalent, to all the other layers. However the linguistic layer model of software is most instructive for an altogether different claim it makes, this time about the fundamental incommensurability between any two points or thresholds on the continuum of layers, and therefore about the difficulty of achieving a collective or "whole" experience. For these are not simply inert technical translations back and forth; there is a privileged moment in which the written becomes the purely machinic and back again. The operating system may exist as an executable on disk, but it also exists phenomenologically as a metaphoric, cybernetic interface: the "desktop." (Of course metaphor is entirely the wrong term for talking about figurative interactivity, but it will have to do for the moment; in the context of gaming I have proposed "allegorithm," a portmanteau of "allegory" and "algorithm," but it too seems slightly awkward for the present discussion.)

Underscoring its allegorical structure, Aarseth refers to this strange condition as the dual nature of the cybernetic sign. As allegory, it is best understood in a larger social context where the forced divorcement between the poetic and the functional, or the private and the public, or process and stasis, is a projection of the agonizing scars of fragmentation and atomization in all layers of social life. The dialectical movement between fluidity and fixity, seen in the internal workings of software where states and state changes carry the day, is precisely the same political problem posed by ideology (the narratives of failure and determinism summarized at the start of the chapter). Software might not be narrative in the strict sense of the word, but it still might have a beginning, middle, and end – to paraphrase Aristotle – even if those narrative moments are recast as mere variables inside the larger world of the software simulation. Thus too might ideology be recast in digital format.

Riven to the core, software is split between language and machine, even if the machinic is primary. And, more importantly, there is a process of mystification or distancing at work which ensures that the linguistic and the machinic are most definitely not the same thing. Indeed, part of the ideological import of software is the creation and maintenance of such a distinction. This leads to my second general observation which has to do with the depth model of representation (introduced above via Chun's "persistence of visual knowledge"): *software is both scriptural and executable*. As already discussed these two modes are often splayed out into a hierarchical model of two or more layers of code: source code is "prior to" a runtime executable; machine languages are "underneath" programming languages; software applications "drive" the user experience, and so on. The relevant section from Aarseth is worth quoting at length due to its clarity and depth.

The dual nature of the cybernetic sign processes can be described as follows: while some signification systems, such as painted pictures and printed books, exist on only one material level (i.e., the level of paint and canvas, or of ink and paper), others exist on two or more levels, as a book being read aloud (ink-paper *and* voice-soundwaves) or a moving picture being projected (the film strip *and* the image on the silver screen). In these latter cases, the relationship between the two levels may be termed *trivial*, as the transformation from one level to the other (what we might call the secondary sign production) will always be, if not deterministic, then at least dominated by the material authority of the first level. In the cybernetic sign transformation, however, the relationship might be termed *arbitrary*, because the internal, coded level can only be fully experienced by way of the external, expressive level. (When inactive, the program and data of the internal level can of course be studied and described as objects in their own right but not as ontological equivalents of their representations at the external level.) Furthermore, what goes on at the external level can be fully understood only in light of the internal. Both are equally intrinsic, as opposed to the extrinsic status of a performance of a play vis-à-vis the play script. To complicate matters, two different expression objects might result from the same code object under virtually identical circumstances. The possibilities for unique or unintentional sign behavior are endless, which must be bad news for the typologists.[10]

Interfaces are thus manifest (as screens or keyboards), but also latent within software as the mediation between internal and external levels, as Aarseth terms them. The difference between "trivial" and "arbitrary" is essentially that between analog representation and digital representation. The analog is only deemed "trivial" because of the perceived obviousness of mimetic congruence using a continuously variable material value (for example, the curvilinear representation of a sound wave). Likewise the digital is deemed "arbitrary" because of the seeming disconnect between an empirical referent and the mathematical approximation of its form using discrete quanta. However both modes, the "arbitrary" included, are governed by what was referred to previously as "technical transcoding without figuration." What makes Aarseth's claim provocative, and indeed what I hope to rearticulate in this chapter, is that the technical, or "arbitrary," transcoding of symbolic systems is in no way whatsoever a theory of inert material determinism. In fact it is the exact opposite: the fact that abstraction and figuration *do* exist in software (the interface metaphor of the "desktop" as functional emanation of source code, or any number of examples cited previously) demonstrates the fundamental indeterminacy of a technological apparatus that is, admittedly, grounded in rote, deterministic mathematical language. It is representation in form, but not in deed, and this is the paradox. It is representation as mathematical recoding, not as any socially or culturally significant process of figuration, yet at the end of the day what emerges is exactly that.

This is what Aarseth means when he says that "the possibilities for unique or unintentional sign behavior are endless." Let me underscore that this needs to be understood not in the "soft" anthropocentric sense of the varying interpretive and cognitive intangibles brought to the table by human agents, but in the "hard" sense of complex material systems and the innumerable combinations that emerge from them. The fetish in Marx is never blamed on the shortcomings of the human mind, even if it follows a logic of misrecognition. We should not do the same with software.

Given that the book is well underway, it is time to pause and reflect again on the question of method first broached in the preface. This book tries to follow a very specific path, one in which the political interpretation of cultural and technical objects is put forth not as one possible style of reading to be swapped in and out according to one's methodological preference, but instead that the political interpretation of cultural and technical objects is essentially synonymous with interpretation itself such that to do one is necessarily to do the other, and likewise to ignore the former is to perform the latter poorly. Software, in other words, *asks a question to which the political interpretation is the only coherent answer.*

Note that this approach is different from those who seek to unmask how this or that piece of software might be a bearer of some political worldview. This is not a theory of *ideologies*, each paired up with an appropriately insightful critique crafted to debunk it. The task here is not to claim that software has a "meaning," political or otherwise, that can be revealed through a convenient methodological scaffolding called the political interpretation. Quite the opposite is the case. A certain networked relation is at play: software, the social, and the act of interpretation combine in "an intense mimetic thicket" and it is this thicket that, in its own elaboration, can be called the political. Chun's claim made at the outset that "software is a functional analog to ideology" contains all of the many strands of this emergent structure: (1) software and ideology are related in a fundamental way; (2) yet it is a relationship of figuration in which the complexities and contradictions of ideology, which itself contains both utopian and repressive instincts, are modeled and simulated out of the formal structure of software itself; (3) further, software is functional and thereby exacerbates and ridicules the tension within itself between the narrative and machinic layers – the strictly functional transcodings of software, via a compiler or a script interpreter for example, fly in the face of the common sense fact that software has both an executable layer, which should obey the rules of a purely functional aspect of the code (similar to what Genette calls the "paratextual" in literature), and a scriptural layer, which would obey the rules of semantics and subjective expression (in Deleuze, remember, it is the *non*subjective that is the machinic).

In fact all this comes under a more common name, *allegory*. The point is not simply that software is functional, but that software's mock resolution of the tension between the machinic and the narrative, the functional and the disciplinary, the fluid and the fixed, the digital and the analog, is an allegorical figure for the way in which these same political and social realities are "resolved" today: not through oppression or false consciousness, as in the orthodox ideological critique, but through the ruthless rule of code, which proposes that the analog should live on to the end, only to show that the analog never existed in the first place. And as writers like Jameson and Northrop Frye have pointed out, the act of interpretation is but another moment of allegorical structuring, as parallel or "analog" discourses are extracted or, if you like, expressed through and within media technologies (or, formerly, within texts). From Plato onwards, such is the logic of ideology. To claim that ideology exists is to claim that political apathy and machinic canalization are present here alongside the very possibility of their transcendence – otherwise it would not be ideology, but something like psychosis. So it is really desire that is the stuff of ideology. It is a desire not for the absence of ideology in something like the end of history, but for the very presence of ideology as a reminder for how the sacred "end" must always already be contained in the profane present. The logic shines through quite elegantly in the words of Ernst

Bloch, writing from an earlier moment in the machine age. "Someone once said that people are in Heaven and don't know it; Heaven certainly still seems somewhat unclear. Leave everything from his statement but the *will* that it be true – then he was right."[11]

3   Are Some Things Unrepresentable?

The New York Times recently published a PowerPoint slide (Fig. 3.1) on its front page taken from a meeting between military leaders and government officials. The slide depicts the American military strategy in Afghanistan in the form of a massive diagram of forces and relations. A marvel of data visualization, the slide is exhaustively detailed. One hundred and twenty nodes, rendered with phrases such as "Tribal Governance" and "Insurgents," are connected together with scores of lines and arrows. Like a flow chart, these lines demonstrate links of influence. Font size indicates the relative importance of each text heading. Color clusters designate broad zones based on themes such as the government, the coalition forces, the population, and the insurgency. Yet the frenzy of words and links begins to overwhelm the eye. It is unclear exactly what the slide is meant to convey or indeed if it is meant to convey anything at all. " 'When we understand that slide, we'll have won the war,' General McChrystal dryly remarked . . . as the room erupted in laughter."[1]

Having such an overwhelming amount of detail, the PowerPoint slide is not easy to digest. In fact, the high level of detail seems to hinder comprehension rather than aid it. Unlike realism in painting or photography, wherein an increase in technical detail tends to bring a heightened sense of reality (at least in the traditional definition of aesthetic realism that has held sway more or less since the Renaissance), the high level of technical detail visible here overwhelms the human sensorium, attenuating the viewer's sense of reality. Rather,

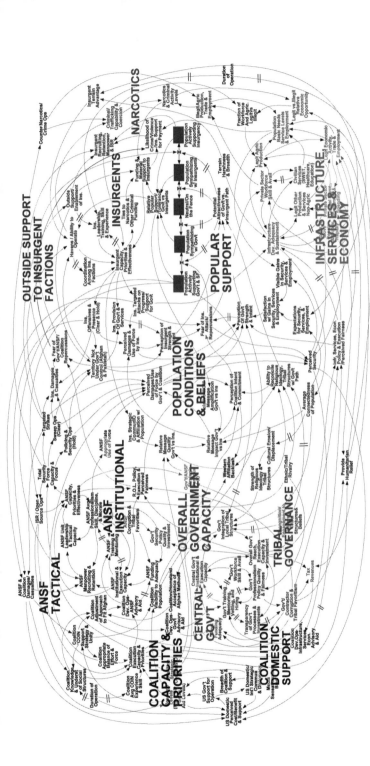

Figure 3.1. PowerPoint slide depicting the American military strategy in Afghanistan. Source: "Dynamic Planning for COIN in Afghanistan," PA Consulting Group, 2009.

like a fractal whose complexity does not decrease when viewed through a magnifying glass, the information contained in the slide does not grow more coherent the longer one inspects it. Eschewing lucidity, the diagram withdraws from the viewer's grasp, effectively neutering its capacity as a vehicle for information. One is left wondering what exactly the slide is meant to communicate. Is it communicating America's military strategy in Afghanistan? Or the reverse, is it communicating how difficult such strategies are to communicate in the first place?

Engaging with McChrystal's image is difficult at first glance. But what would happen if one were to talk about this image in strictly aesthetic terms, as if one were talking about a painting? Would it be possible to view this peculiar brand of visual representation as a work of aesthetics? What would be the result? A painting of military life? An image of a network? Or even an interface into the society of control, to borrow a term from Gilles Deleuze?[2]

Regarding the image in this way is indeed challenging. Even at a purely aesthetic level it is not clear what precisely the image is trying to represent. Is it trying to represent data, an algorithm, a diagram, a system, a network? These terms all seem to connect to each other, yet they mean very different things. Data would be represented very differently from an algorithm, would it not? Yet it would be safe to say that all these terms fall, more or less, under the umbrella of information. Taken in that light, can this image reveal anything interesting about the nature of information aesthetics? Can it tell us anything about the relationship between transparency and concealment? Between representability and unrepresentability?

Entering more deeply into the discussion, we might address the obvious sensory qualities of the image, its use of color, line, and word. The variations in text size inject a sense of scale into the thicket of curves and arrows. The text labels, demarcating network nodes, achieve an appealing texture. No nodes overlap. Occupying its own area of the image, each node is surrounded by a moat of white space. Spread evenly into discrete cells within the frame, they demonstrate what art historian Aloïs Riegl called "tactile" perception. The lines too are well spaced. More like links than mere strokes of a pen, these marks introduce movement into the image. Like a complex vector field, the lines map multiple relationships and hierarchies. Showing what comes first, second, or third within any segment of flow, the lines establish specific connections between parts of the image, while discounting other ones. As if to mitigate the tendencies of the links and the nodes, the seven color clusters – navy blue, light blue, red, black, light green, dark green, and orange – reorganize the entire image into clearly marked zones. These themselves echo the "Green Zones" erected in cities like Baghdad and other global sites under American military control. Even as links flow in and out, the color clusters remain coherent, like city-states organized under federation to an imperial power.

However such a reading of the image can only go so far. Amid all the talk recently of "data" and "information" it becomes more and more difficult to know what these terms mean, or indeed to tell them apart in the first place. Are the nodes meant to represent data, while the links represent information? Is data meant to be textual and static, while information elastically structured via flows and arrangements?

A turn to etymology will provide some rudimentary guidance. The Latin *data*, a participle in the neuter, means literally "the things having been given." Or in short form one might render the term more elegantly as "the givens." French preserves this double meaning nicely by calling data the *données*. As natural gift, as empirical trace, data are not simply measurements or recorded facts, they are also in some sense ontologically raw, not so much thrown into the world, but left over, bare, remaining after the tide of being recedes. So with "data" there is stress on the empirical proffering of measurable or otherwise observable fact that has been given forth. Something has already taken place, and via a gift or endowment, it enters into presence. (Given more time it would be to possible to elaborate the argument, begun in the introduction, that, whereas data have always had a certain *phenomenological* claim, the computer supersedes mere data)

Stemming from a different Latin root, information means the act of taking form or being put into form. So in contrast to data, information stresses less a sense of presence and giving-forth, and more a plastic adoption of shape. Information exists whenever worldly things are "in-formed," or "put into form." As Vilém Flusser put it once in an illustrative vignette, the leaves that fall in the autumn have no information because they are scattered to and fro, but if one puts them into form – for example by moving them around to spell out a word, or simply by raking them into piles – the leaves *gain information*. The worldly things, having previously been given, have now been given form. Thus if data open a door into the realm of the empirical and ultimately the ontological (the level of being), information by contrast opens a door into the realm of the aesthetic.

Neither term can be entirely understood on its own. With this in mind, and since information differs from data in a more immediate and dramatic way, I offer the first of two theses. *Data have no necessary visual form.* But how could this be true? Is the world today not drowning in data visualizations? Is the world not the very embodiment of data made visible? Consider the genre of image-making known as information visualization. Numerous exemplars exist, from John von Neumann's influential flow charts from the 1940s, to the "crude" diagram given in the appendix to Karl Deutsch's *Nerves of Government*, even Freud has a number of network diagrams in his work (and certainly Jacques Lacan and Félix Guattari are full of them), to Edward Tufte's books, or today's ubiquitous "maps of the Internet" (Fig. 3.2), which all seem to resemble a large cauliflower floating free somewhere beyond the solar system.

Evoking such questions is sure to bring controversy. To be sure the first thesis is a very particular one, so let me reiterate it in more verbose language: data, reduced to their purest form of mathematical values, exist first and foremost as number, and, as number, data's primary mode of existence is not a visual one. Thus to say "no necessary" means that any visualization of data requires a contingent leap from the mode of the mathematical to the mode of the visual. This does not mean that aestheticization cannot be achieved. And it does not mean that such acts of aestheticization are unmotivated,

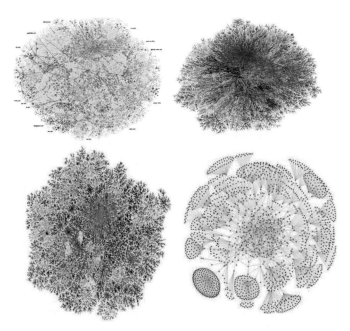

Figure 3.2. Four different maps of the Internet, produced by different methods and sources, selected from numerous examples available via a normal web search.

nugatory, arbitrary, or otherwise unimportant. It simply means that any visualization of data must invent an artificial set of translation rules that convert abstract number to semiotic sign. Hence it is not too juvenile to point out that any data visualization is first and foremost a visualization *of the conversion rules themselves*, and only secondarily a visualization of the raw data.

Visualization wears its own artifice on its sleeve. And because of this, any data visualization will be first and foremost a theater for the *logic of necessity* that has been superimposed on the vast sea of contingent relations. So with the word "form" already present in the predicate of the first thesis, and if the reader will allow a sloppy syllogism, it is possible to rejigger the first thesis so that both data and information may be united in something of an algebraic relationship. Hence now it goes, *data have no necessary information*.

(Enlisting aid from philosophy will help make sense of things. To say that data have no necessary information, that they are formless, existing prior to formation, the mere stuff of the world, the raw material of measurement and nothing more – to say this puts data on the same ontological footing as a number of previous concepts from the history of philosophy including Aristotle's material cause, Spinoza's substance, Whitehead's actual occasions, Badiou's pure multiplicities, or Deleuze's intensities on the surface of the One. These are some sources within philosophy that bear upon the present understanding of data. Likewise to gain a better philosophical context for information one must evoke that other ancient philosophical specter, not so much the purely material realm, but the realm of the eternal form, the realm of spirit, of truth and beauty. Thus in Deleuze information isn't the bubbling chaotic material plane, but rather what Deleuze calls the virtual [which exists with potency across that plane]. But I should specify here too, before moving on, that this first thesis is not an affront to phenomenology, for it does not deny the existence of necessity within givenness. It merely states that form is not logically included within data, in other words, that data may appear without form. The same can not be said about information, of course, a term which in its very etymology is almost tautologically bound up with the concept of form.)

Repetition is the key to my second thesis. For there is but one image, from beginning to end, across the decades, a massive repetition of the same and nothing more: *Only one visualization has ever been made of an information network*, for there can be only one. The reader will thankfully be spared the same kind of scrutiny given previously to the opening image (Fig. 3.1), but suffice it to say that there is a conspicuous uniformity to the scores and scores of images available today advertising a "map of the Internet" (Fig. 3.2), or even a "map of human neural nets" – all of which end up being not so far removed from the "map of the American military strategy in Afghanistan." The hub-and-spoke cloud aesthetic predominates. Miniscule branching structures cluster together forming intricate three-dimensional spaces. Nodes are connected by links. Small capillaries merge into ever greater arteries fabricating massive hierarchies governing flows and prohibitions on flow. Yet through it all, the legibility of the map remains suspiciously one-sided, even ideologically motivated. The viewer is able to intuit certain vague cosmological "facts" about the digital firmament (apparently information likes to cluster; these color enclaves persist unmiscegenated; we love trees after all), while gleaning little about the "facts on the ground" (who is connecting and who isn't; the intranetwork struggles between protocological and proprietary software; the reification of pyramidal hierarchy; monetization of unpaid micro labor). My proposal therefore, in plain language, is that *every map of the Internet looks the same*. Every visualization of the social graph looks the same. A word cloud equals a flow chart equals a map of the Internet. All operate within a single uniform set of aesthetic codes. The size of this aesthetic space is one.[3]

But what does this mean? What are the aesthetic repercussions of such claims? One answer is that no poetics is possible in this uniform aesthetic space. There is little differentiation at the level of formal analysis. We are not all mathematicians after all. One can not talk about genre distinctions in this space, one can not talk about high culture versus low culture in this space, one can not talk about folk vernacular, nor about modernist spurs and other such tendencies. This is why computer culture speaks in terms of icons, and why one might describe today's information aesthetic as a kind of neo-symbolism in which the monochromatic multiplicity of symbols has engulfed all else. A single symbolic code reigns, iterated universally. And where there is only one, there is nothing. For a representation of the one is, in fact, a representation of nothing.

Every interface must try to overcome its own unworkability. So let me restate the two theses side by side, that they may be collided and compared. Thesis 1, *data have no necessary visual form*; thesis 2, *only one visualization has ever been made of an information network*. There is indeed a dialectical tension between these two theses, for if there is no necessary connection, why do so many network visualizations look the same? There must be some kind of mandate somewhere that prohibits alternate aesthetic modes. What is the origin of such a mandate?

Each thesis pulls against the other. On the one hand, thesis 1 argues for digital aesthetics as nothing. On the other, thesis 2 argues for digital aesthetics as one. Either data offer zero help as to how they ought to be aestheticized, or they eclipse all available possibilities under a single way of seeing. One might assign a name to this curious contradiction and call it the dilemma of *unrepresentability* lurking within information aesthetics. There is a cognitive dissonance between theses 1 and 2. My goal here is not to do away with such dissonance, nor should we waste time trying to resolve it. Its function is to shed a light on the logic of unrepresentability, something which emerges as a strategy existing through and across the two theses. Thesis 1 proves that representation *must* take place, while thesis 2 makes sure that when it takes place it *says nothing*. Hence the middle is lost. Only the two ends of the chain remain. At one extreme, information aesthetics fails because it is unable to take alternative forms, escaping from the shadow of the predominant form. At the other extreme, information aesthetics fails because it adopts one form at the expense of all others. Mediation is missing. There is, in a very literal sense, *no media happening here*.

New media demonstrate, then, that the augmentation of functional or algorithmic efficiency goes hand in hand with a decline in symbolic efficiency. Hence the following law: an increase in aesthetic information produces a decline in information aesthetics.

Algorithmic interfaces – even as they flaunt their own highly precise, virtuosic levels of detail – prove that something is happening behind and beyond the visible. In other words, *there are some things that are unrepresentable*. And the computer is our guide into that realm.

New media have not often been drawn into the larger discourse of unrepresentability. The position described thus far is something of an outlier. Other authors writing on the topic have framed it rather differently, often in terms of photography. "Are Some Things Unrepresentable?" is the title of an essay by the French philosopher Jacques Rancière.[4] He and many others today are engaged in a loose debate around the power of the image, around the future of the image. They ask whether it is possible to depict violence in images. They ask what happens when graphic images of state-sponsored torture circulate within the mass media. They ask what do pictures want, and can an image *kill*?[5]

As sense is redistributed into different arrangements, different "regimes" of art will emerge. Rancière calls it a distribution of the sensible. The regime known as representation is only one specific regime for Rancière, a regime produced by certain historical and social realities. In other words, representation is bound by a specific distribution of the sensible. Within this framework, he asserts that there are two basic representational situations. The first, which is triggered by what he calls the "internal impossibility of representation," champions the "straightforward tale" that comes unadorned and lacking in artifice.[6] He associates this mode with Plato and Plato's ethical framework for art. The second, arising from the "indignity" of representation, takes up the call of "sublime art" and tries, even in the face of failure, to "record the trace of the unthinkable."[7] This he associates with the more modern notions of the Kantian and even Burkean sublime. So unrepresentability – and here is Rancière's trick – is less a question of the failures of representation on its own terms and more a question of the historical shift out of one regime into a subsequent regime. Anti-representation arises, he argues, with the advent of an "aesthetic revolution" inaugurating a new regime labeled the "aesthetic." The hallmark of the aesthetic regime is a breakdown between subjects and art: "There are no longer rules of appropriateness between a particular subject and a particular form, but a general availability of all subjects for any artistic form whatsoever."[8] Thus the aesthetic regime shares much with the profanation or secularization of culture that takes place particularly during the modern period, sometimes called simply the nihilism of modernity. But the regime is not incompatible with postmodernism and the so-called "end of master narratives," which itself pronounces a grand leveling of all value into one transcultural soup. On this point, then,

Rancière quite correctly points out that the opposite of representation is *not* non-figuration, which is to say not modernism. Instead he suggests that one might look to realism for the most non-representational form, for in realism everything is leveled and equally representable, and "this 'equally representable' spells the ruin of the representative system."[9]

Violence takes center stage now, for the dramatic consequences of this line of thinking concern the Shoah and the ability or inability for the Holocaust to be represented in art. Rancière places two literary excerpts side by side, a passage from Robert Antelme's *The Human Race* on daily life at Buchenwald and a passage from one of the great works of literary realism, Flaubert's *Madame Bovary*. The language is strikingly similar, a paratactic style of lists of unconjoined phrases and flat observations. "The concentration camp experience as lived by Robert Antelme, and the invented sensory experience of Charles and Emma [Bovary], are conveyed according to the same *logic of minor perceptions* added to one another, which makes sense in the same way, through their silence, through their appeal to a minimal auditory and visual experience."[10] The problem therefore with the question of representing the Holocaust is precisely not that of representation itself, which is to say the difficulty of being able to put something into words. Ineffability is not the problem. "The problem is in fact rather the reverse," Rancière argues. "The language that conveys this experience *is in no way specific to it*."[11] In other words it is not an impossible language, nor is it a specific language. (Suggesting, perhaps even more provocatively, that it is *possible* and *generic*.) There is no special literary style that is as unusual and special that it can only be used in a rendering of life in the concentration camp. In a certain sense this is another way of understanding the notion of the "banality of evil," which we owe to the work of Hannah Arendt. For Rancière such banality illustrates the rift between two grand modes of mediation, on the one hand the specificity of representation, and on the other the genericness of the aesthetic.

About representation and the aesthetic, Rancière is essentially correct. And even if it is something of a trick, he is also essentially correct when he says that unrepresentability means the shift into the aesthetic. Nevertheless there exists a slightly different view waiting to be aired regarding this type of discourse, the type of discourse that roots unrepresentability firmly in questions of political violence (for which the Holocaust is the most significant test).

Not explicitly referencing many of the canonical texts, Rancière's essay still clearly shares a number of things with other authors' work on similar topics. For example, one could make a connection to Susan Sontag's books *On Photography* (1977) and *Regarding the Pain of Others* (2003), as well as Judith Butler's recent essay responding to Sontag, "Torture and the Ethics of Photography: Thinking with Sontag."[12] One might also consider the documentary film made by Sontag in 1974 called *Promised Lands*, which examines the ongoing Arab-Israeli conflict and specifically the question of violence and how violence may or may not be put into photographic or cinematic form. Likewise there is Harun Farocki's stunning film *Images of the World and the Inscription of War* (1988). Or even Georges Didi-Huberman's book first published in French in 2003, *Images in Spite of All: Four Photographs from Auschwitz*, which deals with the question of photography in the camps.[13] "Unrepresentability poses a question which can only be answered via specific kinds of violence" – this is the discourse that needs to be fleshed out today. Ultimately, it is possible to agree with this conclusion, but on very different terms. And in fact in order to arrive at a similar destination it shall be necessary to take a number of detours not anticipated by Rancière and perhaps not endorsed by him either.

The main difficulty with Rancière's position, and those sympathetic to him whether implicitly or explicitly, is that the question is in fact never exclusively one of representability. The question is one of affective response. Would photographs of suffering move us? And if we are not moved, are we to blame? Rancière's concern therefore is one of ethical obligation, never simply that of representation and representability (barring for the moment those specific traditions such as Platonism – and Rancière is certainly not a Platonist – wherein representation and ethical obligation are intimately intertwined).[14] Occasionally he plays the part of the nervous liberal, worried whether certain images will escape into the wild, and if they do whether or not the spectators witnessing them will exhibit the proper emotional responses. His position is therefore at root allied with the creation and maintenance of proper subject positions. His is a discourse of visual culture that is quite familiar: the power of an image relies exclusively on its circulation as hidden or visible; images exist either as triggers for emotional responses within populations, or as cynical evidence of that same population's numbness to them. Either seen or unseen, either affecting or impotent – such is the trap of representation today.[15]

Given Rancière's axiom – that unrepresentability ethically obligates us to discuss images of political violence – and in order to outline an alternative solution, consider again the opening comments concerning data visualization. In comparison to political violence data visualization seems trivial indeed. We are now not speaking about the wanton destruction of real lives, of the black inhumanity of the camps. The point is not to argue for the superiority of "informatic violence" over that of political violence. Even to pose the debate in such terms confuses much and explains very little.

Abu Ghraib or the Twin Towers might dominate today's debate. But the point is to consider a regime of art that does not appear much at all in Rancière, nor in the work of others like Butler who have weighed in on the question of political violence in photography. (If it appears anywhere it appears in Deleuze.) Consider then the *control* regime, a social and aesthetic framework that has its own brand of violence, if not as singularly spectacular as Abu Ghraib or the Twin Towers, or as catastrophically ruthless as the modern machinery of the Holocaust, then at least insidious and pervasive in its own particular deployment. If we are indeed living inside what Deleuze called the society of control, are we not obligated to reflect on the violence embedded in *that* kind of society, to reflect on what it would mean for *that* kind of violence to be represented or unrepresented? Would this offer an alternative response to Rancière's axiom?

Regarding the control regime, I merely proffer a single speculative claim here, leaving a more detailed examination of the concept to other writings. Let this serve as a kind of descriptive provocation, not meant to be definitive and no doubt slightly unsatisfactory. One of the key consequences of the control society is that *we have moved from a condition in which singular machines produce proliferations of images, into a condition in which multitudes of machines produce singular images.* As evidence for the first half of this thesis consider the case of the cinematic or photographic camera, a singular device with the ability to output thousands and thousands of images in constant mutation. Hence Rancière's concerns are valid within their own domain, bounded as they are by the paradigmatic examples of photography and cinema.[16] As evidence for the second half consider the case of Wikipedia, a singular (data) image produced by thousands and thousands of end users on their laptops. Or consider the network visualizations evoked above, a singular aesthetic form produced by scores of uncoordinated network scientists and web designers. In its very resistance toward being put into an image it demonstrates the singularity of the image today, at the hands of a multitude of machines. There is quite literally an inability to render the network as an image differentiated from other images. There is a single image and thus there is none.

Digital media require a different assessment of violence and unrepresentability. Those who wring their hands over the supposed unrepresentability of images of state-sponsored torture or other political violence exhibit a curious form of blindness toward the apparatus. They exhibit a form of blindness toward the mode of production, sublimating a political worry, noble as it may be, into an observation about art. Of course it is important to think about violence, and to confront it directly. It is only natural to wish for *some* mechanical link between images and violence. It would be a noble pursuit if it were not demonstrably false: the photos from the Abu Ghraib prison were released, or they were not (and nothing changed); we grieved and we protested in the proper channels, or we did not (and still nothing changed). Representation *happened*, even if one feels anxiety about the outcome. The problem is that adequate visualizations of control society have *not happened*. Representation has not happened. At least not yet.

Each photograph of violence is a testament to the represent-ability of violence, not its unrepresentability. So what went wrong with the analysis? How did it get off track? At this point it is wise to return to first principles, recalling that the consti-tutive axis for representation always has a relationship with the mode of production, not simply the ideological conceits and tricks of state power that are its epiphenomena. Thus if unrepresentability is in play it will be in play around the mode of production and the realities of the socio-historical situation. It will govern the logic of showing and hiding the economic base. Or if one prefers more Freudian language, consider how in a dream the thing that will be represented most fla-grantly is the very thing that will be, in practical terms, the most invisible. Consider the logic of how the thing that most permeates our daily lives will be the same thing that retreats from any tangible malleability in our hands and minds. But what are these things? We must speak of the information economy. We must simply describe today's mode of produc-tion in its many divergent details: the diffusion of power into distributed networks, the increase in local autonomous decision making, the ongoing destruction of the social order at the hands of industry, the segmentation and rationalization of minute gestures within daily life, the innovations around unpaid micro labor, the monetization of affect and the "social graph," the entrainment of universalizing behaviors within protocological organization – *these* are the things that are unrepresentable. And are they not also harbingers of a new pervasive and insidious social violence? To speak of the trumped-up CNN spectacles of military porn in hallowed, hushed voices as some sort of affront to the truth of represen-tation is to miss the point entirely. Cast it all away. The point of unrepresentability is the point of power. And the point of power today is not in the image. The point of power today resides in networks, computers, algorithms, information, and data. Some may deny this last point, yet it is impossible to deny it and remain a materialist.

One crucial question remains: How to represent power today? Countervailing tendencies already exist in parallel to the opening PowerPoint slide, refuting and rejecting it. For just as network visualization can tend to obfuscate its own data, it may also reveal systems of organization and power, given the right conditions. Perhaps most well known are the large format maps drawn by artist Mark Lombardi, maps that reveal with obsessive detail the intricate interconnectedness of systems of power. Likewise consider the stunning information maps produced by the Paris-based group Bureau d'études (Fig. 3.3), large diagrams with titles like "Psy-war Bio-war," "Complex

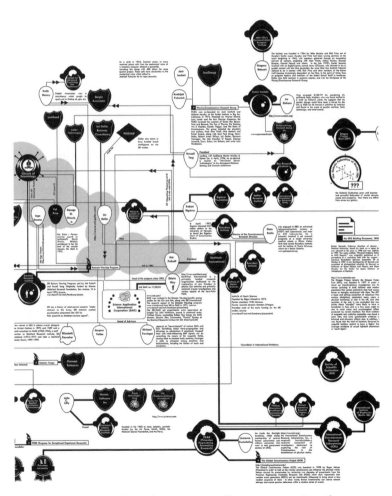

Figure 3.3. Bureau d'Etudes. *Psy-war Bio-war*, 2003. Detail.

of the Self," and "Governing by Networks," which spotlight
flows of influence peddling and back room power grabs. Inter-
estingly these works tend to intervene at the level of "content"
rather than "form" – to rely on an old cliché. While the work
of Bureau d'études is complex and variegated, a number of
their maps tend to follow the flow chart style previously discussed. Thus one must rely exclusively on the data contained
therein. Research-driven and revelatory, their work denudes
the apparatuses of power by showing the deep interconnectedness of business, government, and the elite. The promise of
this approach also finds form in the work of Brian Holmes,
both via his writings and his work as a lecturer and educator.
Holmes, who has written on Bureau d'études as well as other
themes including networked resistance and psychogeography,
offers something like a counter-cartography of information in
which the given protocols of informatic imagination are rigor-
ously tested. These interventions are significant not so much
because they escape the dilemma of unrepresentability – in
fact they tend to confirm my second thesis above on the "one-
ness" of network visualization – but because they launch a new
set of initiatives, shackled not to the obfuscatory power of
network visualization, but to its latent pedagogical and mobi-
lizing potential. But we must be wary of trying to seek redemption in these counter-cartographies, for as the two theses above
demonstrate, the ideological content of the map is ultimately
beholden to the affordances and prohibitions of its form. To
end, then, let us not tarry with the various attempts to critique
the social map at the level of data, and instead consider some
of the attempts to critique it at the level of information.

Frank Gehry's Stata Center, a crisp new university building,
opened on the MIT campus in 2004 (Fig. 3.4). Forms cascade
on top of other forms, producing, through the interstices of
haphazard movement, a fresco of deformation frozen in time.
In Gehry's words, the building "looks like a party of drunken
robots got together to celebrate."[17] Yet not long after the ribbon
cutting a number of design failures began to be noticed by
those using the structure. Of course there is a noble tradition
throughout architectural history of signature buildings leaking,

Figure 3.4. Frank Gehry (architect), Stata Center, Massachusetts Institute of Technology, Cambridge, MA.

cracking, or otherwise failing to live up to the basic necessities of good engineering. Apparently the Stata Center was suffering from the same fate, for the building began to fail in various ways, so much so that the university sued Gehry in 2007 for alleged design and construction shortcomings.

The irony is clear: Gehry has built his reputation on a very specific form of aestheticize breakage, yet here he is blamed for his buildings breaking. He was hired to make forms that appear to fall apart, yet here they are actually falling apart. His "aesthetic failure" arises from a reaction to the minimalism and functionalism of the International Style of architectural modernism. But the notion of his alleged design failures is a paradoxical one. For as the MIT administration would attest, even if an architectural design is allowed to crack and buckle at the semiotic or symbolic level, it is not allowed to fail at the level of material functionality. Walls may bend or warp in deconstructivist architecture, but they cannot crack. In short, failures in function may not appear as function proper; to the extent that they appear at all, they must be transmuted into aesthetic expression, their "breakage" having already been defanged and rearranged into entirely different outcomes. (The contrapositive phenomena exists in another notoriously leaky building, Le Corbusier's Villa Savoye: the leaks are true failures in function, housed within a modernist style that prohibits failures in form; these may be thought of as "honest" failures in function, whereas Gehry's are disingenuous.)

Honest informatic failures – failures of function – if they are pleasurable or "artistic" in any way, are typically recast under a purely aesthetic aegis. Hence there exist a number of artists creating beauty via the corruption of function, from Jean Tinguely's kinetic sculpture, to the flicker films of Tony Conrad, or the programmatic drawings of Sol LeWitt, or the computer art of Jodi.org.

Enlisting such artists at this point in the discussion serves a specific purpose, for there is evidence here of an approach to information visualization different from those mentioned thus far. For Gehry, whether or not one insists on labeling him a deconstructivist, the impetus comes from the fundamentally poststructuralist nature of the information age in which no formal data are immune from their own corruption from within, modulating the formerly clean internal scaffolding into warped surface arcs and organic "blobs" born of algorithmic iteration. (That Gehry reportedly designs by hand using wooden blocks and crumpled paper is a red herring; these buildings are unthinkable without the computer, just as Sullivan's skyscrapers were unthinkable without the steel mills.) Or for Tinguely or Conrad it is the machine itself that rears forward, proving that the pure mechanical sequence of things, if it is blocked or redirected, can shine through as elemental experience. Or LeWitt or Jodi, who in divergent and incompatible ways nevertheless both deploy code in such a way that it appears as non-code.

Art works like these can be glorious, but a bit of skepticism is necessary, since such work does not probe functional informatics as such, merely the point at which functional informatics might be transformed into some delight for the senses. In general, Gehry and these other artists merely *feign* to break the machine, all the while restaging it as broken beauty. While tarrying with the algorithmic, each ultimately sacrifices the algorithmic in favor of the aesthetic. None of these artists is creating new data types, new "if-then" statements, new network diagrams, new syllogisms, or new mathematical functions *for their own sake*. The artists may experiment with systematicity or functionalism, as many conceptual artists have done, but always ultimately to revert such machinic realities to the staid structures of fine art.[18] They turn the machine into art, but never art into machine – and when at rare moments the latter does come to fruition, it does so only under the sad and cynical banner of "the art factory," be it that of Andy Warhol a generation ago or Jeff Koons today.

Looping back now, we have come full circle from the law of information aesthetics mentioned previously. Gehry, Jodi, and the others enact the law, only in reverse: the triumph of the aesthetic precipitates a decline in informatic perspicuity. An increase in information aesthetics produces a decline in aesthetic information. Yet regardless if the law is read forward or backward, one is still locked in the trap of unrepresentability.

Gehry's building is a sign of the times. It helps reveal the basic conundrum explored here, which one may summarize according to three basic moments in cultural production and interpretation. While trying to give form to data, (1) network scientists and web designers have tended to aestheticize pure systematicity, thereby sacrificing the aesthetic in favor of the algorithmic, as evidenced by the many "maps of the Internet." Yet (2) others like Gehry or Jodi feign to break the machine and re-stage it as broken beauty, thereby sacrificing the algorithmic in favor of the aesthetic. While the latter is a great improvement over the former, neither option is ultimately sufficient. They require (3) a remapping of the very terms of representability within the society of control, such that both terms return to their proper home, the socio-political realities that have produced them in the first place.

Overtures are scored with certain motifs meant to reappear. One of my themes was that the constitutive axis for representation always has a relationship with the mode of production. The problem today, however, is that this axis is broken. (Was it ever not?) That is to say, we do not yet have a critical or poetic language in which to represent the control society.

Returning to methodology, I cite again Jameson's technique for remapping the social. With much of the book exhausted, it is now possible to say more about it. "Cognitive mapping," defined as the attempt to achieve provisional orientation with the social totality, is described in a number of Jameson's texts, particularly his two books on film. Cognitive mapping emerges from a historical contradiction "in which the truth of our social life as a whole – in Lukács' terms, as a totality – is increasingly irreconcilable with the possibilities of aesthetic expression or articulation available to us."[19] The cognitive map is enlisted, Jameson explains, "to enable a situational representation on the part of the individual subject to that vaster and properly unrepresentable totality which is the ensemble of society's structures as a whole."[20] One of the reasons why this method is so useful is that it does not allow the state to dictate the terms of the debate, as any meditation on political violence (Abu Ghraib, Guantanamo Bay, the Twin Towers) would tend to do. Instead Jameson's method places the responsibility firmly at the feet of history, allowing the socio-historical situation, which of course may include the vicissitudes of political violence but is never determined by them, engulf the subject, inflating and inflecting his or her representations of the present.

Information interfaces, particularly the many attempts to "map" information, often come up short on this score, for they typically offer little orientation within the social totality. Worse, they often exacerbate the problem by veiling it behind candy-colored lines and nodes. The tools and techniques required to create cognitive maps of the information society are scarcely evident even today. Hence the need, I suggest, for "allegories of control" as figurative aids for understanding today's control society. Jameson would never say that the opening image of military strategy (Fig. 3.1) is a map of a system. He would say the image is *an allegory for* a map of a system. The difference is slight but crucial. Yet the point is not so much to call for a return to cognitive mapping, which of course is of highest importance, but to call for *a poetics as such* for this mysterious new machinic space.

The *logos* has no contrary – as Foucault famously said, and later famously retracted. He was wrong when he said it in relationship to the mad, but perhaps it carries some truth today in relationship to the machine. Today's systemics have no contrary. Algorithms and other logical structures are uniquely, and perhaps not surprisingly, monolithic in their historical development. There is one game in town: a positivistic dominant of reductive, systemic efficiency and expediency. Offering a counter-aesthetic in the face of such systematicity is the first step toward building a poetics for it, a language of representability adequate to it.

Here many challenges remain. But while unearthing alternatives might seem difficult, once the first few steps are taken, a wide-open plane emerges, a vast anti-history of informatics waiting to be written, a vast world of representation waiting to be inscribed. To create a poetics for such algorithmic systems is the first step, necessary but not sufficient, in the quest to *represent* them.

Miles of canyon separating the none from the one, such is the dilemma of unrepresentability. On the one hand the "no necessary" trap of the first thesis, which demotes all things under heaven to the same unformed fate, binds the world with shackles of cynicism and relegates every life to the cybernetic struggle of all against all. On the other hand the "only one" trap of the second thesis, which imbues a single power player (the mode of production) with totalizing command, funnels the polyphonic desiring forces into a monochromatic channel of indentured expression. Lack of light will blind representation, but excess of light will dazzle it. Between these two mountains lies the antinomy of the material. The problem of unrepresentability, thus, lies stuck in the gorge of the world. To that place we must return if ever Rancière's question is to be answered: *Are some things unrepresentable?*

4 Disingenuous Informatics

Is *24* a Political Show?

Distinguishing between competing interpretations has always been the domain of hermeneutics. When interpreting culture, one must necessarily contend with the problem of meaning. What can be said coherently about any given cultural artifact? Is the artifact always forthright about expressing what it means? Or is the artifact dealing in figurative or allegorical expression, making reference to a parallel, alternate narrative? What is the "best" technique for hunting down such a parallel narrative? Must we all become vigilant audience members, carefully substituting readings for or against any given manifest clue, in order that the latent narrative may see the light of day?

I have tried to address some of these questions in previous chapters, often in a more theoretical register. Certain emblematic games or images have played a role thus far. But in this chapter we will zoom in and consider a specific case study, a single media artifact within interface culture. Not ostensibly digital, this artifact will nevertheless serve as useful instruction for the ways in which the protocological regime saturates the most far-flung corners of cultural production.

Games and images are not the same though, and must be interpreted in different ways. The same may be said for television, despite my quest here for a new master code to unlock interface culture in general. Indeed television also demands a mode of interpretation specially tailored to it. For instance, there is a common sense notion that 24, the television drama broadcast on Fox from 2001 to 2010, is a show that says something about contemporary life. Roughly stated, the conventional wisdom on 24 is that "the show *is* America." Set in post-September-eleventh America, the hour-long serial is a prism into the nation itself, its anxieties about terrorism and torture, the growing police state, an obsession over real-time phenomena, the security of the clan and the family, the power of information systems, and the like. In recent years the show has provoked a flurry of controversy around these and other hot button political debates.

Is 24 a political show? Whether an inspection of Fox's ideological bias adequately describes the inner workings of this particular cultural artifact remains to be seen. However I would like to pose it as a problem for critique: Is 24 political, and if so in what ways is it political? How does this particular cultural artifact express a political claim? What hermeneutic method is appropriate to interpret the "meaning" of 24 in the digital age?

"24 is essentially propaganda." Such is the indictment most commonly heard from the left. As propaganda, 24 serves an ideological role for pro-administration hawks in the United States keen on shoring up the image of the Department of Homeland Security, the war against terror, the repeal of *habeas corpus*, and so on. After all, the show is produced by Fox, a right-wing television network, and endorsed by Rush Limbaugh and other members of the right elite. Alternately there are those who point to the show as a form of public vetting of current debates, such as the interpretation of the show's second season as a vital, contemporaneous critique of the faulty intelligence that lead up to the 2003 Iraq War. Further, some point to the show as wish fulfillment of a certain progressive flavor, the election of the first black president, or contrariwise as wish fulfillment from the other side of the aisle altogether, the absolute elevation of the executive branch over the juridical and congressional branches, themselves rendered impotent and invisible.

A common conclusion, then, is that 24 is performing political work within culture, in that it advocates a utilitarian moral philosophy that pits dubious short-term actions (e.g. torture) against the "greater good" of the contemporary state. If the new millennium brings a novel spin to the utilitarian impulse it is probably the way in which a teleological sense of total utility is concocted anew with both a tick-tock urgency and a military state in which the "maximized good" subsumes the very horizon of moral truth. Utopia or fascism? It is hard to tell which. Two camps become evident, each with its own strategies and virtues. On one side, the sense of urgency is a natural sublimation of the information age, to be sure, in which networked instantaneousness is the expected norm: any political "solution" is chronologically dependent only on the computer cycles available to execute it. The challenges in 24 are always "informatic" in this sense, because they hinge on the abilities of various cybernetic systems (weapon, com-link, agent, satellite camera) to operate smoothly without obstruction. But on the other side, whence does the show derive its yen for the definition of the total moral frame as that of the security of the state – at any cost – against total annihilation? Is this not also the consummate late-modern anxiety, that those threats which hitherto arrived in many shades of grey have now become, like the computer itself, *binary*, as in the nuclear holocaust of the Cold War, or the terror strike, or the viral pandemic, or the warming of the planet, which promise to arrive not with small pricks of pins and needles but with a total collapse without recourse.

Like a symptom indicating a deeper structure, the utilitarian moral philosophy appears via a number of narrative and formal details. The most common is the digital clock, both in the nondiegetic time code that appears regularly before and after each commercial interruption and from time to time during narrative action, but also with in-world clocks connected to ticking bombs of some sort or another (the nuke in season two, the virus pods in season three, the gas canisters in season five, etc.). There is always a ticking clock in the show. Clocks are adept at heightening the persuasiveness of the utilitarian rationale, for they convincingly elevate the absolute importance of the teleological good over the necessary blood that must be spilled in order to get there. If the end of society is so near, in seconds and minutes even, who will notice a little bit of spilt milk? Even President Palmer, one of the show's few characters not guided solely by the utilitarian impulse, confesses: "Sometimes you have to do the wrong thing for the right reason."[1] (This is what philosophers of utilitarianism call consequentialism, the theory that what makes an action right or wrong are its consequences.)

Marxist theory becomes useful here, particularly the question of totality. For in Marxist theory "totality," echoed later by Georg Lukács as simply the "whole," was an indicator for political consciousness: as capital evolves via fragmentation and isolation, thus progressive thought must totalize both spatially and systemically but also chronologically via reference to "historical" wholes. The teleological quality of utilitarianism as utopia, in the form of thinking about the total security of the population or the future good in broad strokes, is thus at first blush a positive development. It evokes the extremely valuable task, in a very general sense, of obtaining a knowledge of future desires in terms of the material present. This is a version of totality which is closely allied with achieving a progressive social consciousness. In *24*, however, no such thing happens. In a sort of "transfer of affect," any viable consciousness of the social totality is transferred in the show over to the absolute totality of the moral claim: first that "we must save innocent lives" (the utopian, biopolitical claim), which leads directly to the second claim that "we must stop the terrorists at all costs" (the fascistic, utilitarian claim). All intermediate crimes therefore – murder, suspension of juridical rights – are absolved and erased by the moral telos. Totality defines the horizon of truth by virtue of the moral claim itself, and, across this horizon, defines a new set of expedient "realities on the ground" that fit into such an image of the situation.

Allow me to cut to the chase: we are speaking now about capitalism. The utilitarian position is most interesting not so much for the expedient solutions it proposes but for the way in which it prohibits alternate moral frames. This mirrors capitalism's indomitable strength in prohibiting alternative modes of production. The fixity of specific economies and flows, the logical destiny that this or that must happen no matter what the injury, the militarization of everyday life, the alienation of the here and now in exchange for some profiting to be realized later – such is the ideological framework of millennial American capitalism saturating the show's moral infrastructure. Fundamentally it concerns the inability to think or dream in a non-economic manner. This is the way in which the utilitarian claim speaks to "totality." But what sorts of alternate frames? Certainly pacifism has been evacuated as a possible moral frame, or altruism or any sense of romanticism. Barring the saccharine subplots concerning the reuniting of various Counter Terrorist Unit (CTU) family members, there is no inner life in this story, no feeling of interiority, no longing for communion with humanity. But ironically it is also the moral frame of universalism that must too fall by the wayside. The expediency of utilitarianism, at least in the militarized and biopolitical form evident in *24*, is one that claims that there *are* no absolutes. For this is the only way in which short-term crimes can be absolved by long-term solutions. Any action is okay today, as long as it is efficient and expedient in the long run. But is this not also the moral relativism of capitalism, that those quaint pre-modern values such as family, justice, or the integrity of the individual, must be cast off for 'round-the-clock attention to the bottom line? Thus the single moral claim, that the whole must endure, brings about its inversion, in the absolute erosion of ethical action minute-by-minute. (On this point, it has always puzzled me that conservatives accuse postmodernists of being moral relativists, when it is so clearly capitalism that has brought on the moral disintegration they so righteously oppose; that their moral indignation is often paired with a pro-business stance only adds to the confusion.)

Crucial yet elusive, "totality" in *24* has a double if not triple life. Totality refers to the singular utilitarian frame, which must be asserted globally in order to vaporize any sense of experiential moral holism at the human level. But a different notion of totality also exists, the Marxian notion that the whole must always be brought to the fore if one is to make any coherent sense of social life. Into this new, cognitive totality is reflected the logic of all the rest – and, with any luck, an indication of the hermeneutic process required to achieve such a cognitive totality in the first place, replete as it is with all the necessary gaps and hiccups of doing interpretive work.

However, the utilitarian reading leads quite briskly to a second kind of reading, which can be labeled "circumvention of protocol," or more euphemistically "hacking." In a general sense protocol refers to the instigation of material governance within information systems, in a manner entirely distinct from any notion of commercial or juridical power.[2] This is where a specifically anti-capitalist desire blossoms in 24. The show happily rejects existing structures of law and bureaucracy, even as it flaunts its own counter-structure. The utilitarian moral telos, which might be evaluated as fascistic in itself, nevertheless endorses alternative principles of personal virtue, such as will-to-power, instinct, cutting through the red tape, bucking the powers-that-be in order to get the job done. Structure is always what must be circumvented in 24, and it is typically the show's central character, Jack Bauer, who performs such circumvention. Jack is a rogue, never a bureaucrat. In being a rogue, he exhibits an informatic logic, a hacker praxis that is entirely congruent with the waning of modern bureaucracies. In the control society informatic systems are always in a state of "self-exploitation." This means that the informatic system is specifically defined not as an integral object, but as a flexible network of command and control which is only actualized through its own transgression by another informatic force. The force might be a virus, a CTU hacker, or any other informatic agent. So while there is a total, pervasive structure of organization – the total state of war, the militarization of the police, SWAT teams outside every door, automatic weapons, C4 explosives, pervasive militarism of all sectors of life – this is the very same cycle of control that also facilitates "going dark" in the form of the "state of exception," black prisons, extradition, and so on. Protocol is always followed to a tee. There is an extreme attention to craft. The show fetishizes team work and the chain of command. But protocol is also what must always be circumvented. In fact this mode of individuation, with its ebb and flow, is part of what *defines* informatic spaces. In the end breaking the rules is always, always done to achieve better efficiency, whether toward the utilitarian, biopolitical moral end or ultimately the security of the population. Is this utopia or fascism? Again, it is not so clear.

"Just let me do my job"

Is 24 a political show? The question has still not been completely addressed. The various moral claims only go so far. So for a first salvo, I propose a renaming of the series: 24/7. And likewise an assertion, if not evocative then at least provocative: CTU is the sweatshop of the new millennium.

New media and postfordism have a special relationship with one another. The characters on 24 need to be understood not simply as a paramilitary force, what Louis Althusser calls the repressive state apparatus, but also as a postfordist labor force. These are employees who quite literally *cannot clock out*. Like a sweatshop, they are chained to their jobs. Such a constraint is demonstrated in the basic premise of the show, that the work day is no longer nine to five, but extends throughout all twenty-four hours. The show's "day" is a work day. It is a state of exception, but never just a political one. It is an economic state of exception, wherein the normal rules of fair labor practice (periodic work breaks, personal injury protection, overtime pay) are tossed out the window, and willingly so by the employees in question. Reification under modernity was always "I'm just doing my job" – leave me alone in my penance, I'm just "working for the weekend." But reification in the information age has an entirely different emphasis: "Just let me do my job." In this mode there is a heightened ownership of one's labor within an ethic of self-worth and spiritual achievement. It is an appeal: *let* me. Real life is an anti-labor blockade, an interruption. The goal is not to uncouple from the sphere of labor, but instead to enter it entirely and sincerely. Inefficient extra- and inter-labor distractions must be cast off. "Just let me do my job, ok?" – these words are spoken out loud in almost every episode.

Existing in the "exceptional" form of the sweatshop, CTU also appears as a "normal" labor environment. These two are mutually related. The exceptional is always articulated via the normal and vice versa. The sleek corporate feel of the contemporary work space is everywhere in the show. Laptops, cell phones, open cubicles, conference rooms, and multipurpose spaces are signifiers of the post-dotcom renovation of corporate life. Everything is fluid and flexible. Everything is nomadic and impermanent. The explosion at CTU in season two is illustrative of the temporary nature of all contemporary work space. Under postfordism it is common for employees to work in physical conditions that are perpetually "under construction." Members of a work team might have to vacate their jobs on a moment's notice. 24's workers are a postfordist, nomadic labor force left with little to no job security.

Spaces of total surveillance populate the show. The "normal" work environment is the panoptic work environment, and CTU is no exception. Employee communications are able to be monitored at all times, and non-work phones are prohibited at the workplace. Employees are routinely "fire walled" on the show, their work stations surreptitiously quarantined and scrutinized. If all else fails, the office can also always be "locked down" at any time for an internal investigation. The sweatshop logic and the panoptic logic thus coincide in this exceedingly normal labor environment as workers are cuffed to their chairs, inspected on all sides by cameras and intelligent algorithms.

A chief irony in all of this is that the CTU lineup is not very good at doing its job. Each looming catastrophe that drives the show's serial narrative fails to be averted by this crack team: season two, the nuke detonates; five, hostages die, the gas is released; one, the Palmer assassination attempt goes forward; four, meltdown, Air Force One down; three, a spurt of white stuff as the virus vials pop. Catastrophe is, in the narrative logic of 24, the money shot. It *must* be shown.

Routinely frustrated from achieving their goals, nevertheless the slacker nineties are gone forever for these workers. A new totality of work dominates that trumps all other realms of life – desire, justice before the law, personal relationships, and so on. In fact there is effectively *no* domestic space on this show at all. All sexual or familial relationships transpire within the walls of CTU headquarters (Nina/Jack, Kim/Jack, Nina/Tony, Michelle/Tony, Kim/Chase, Angela/Chase), or they transpire within the context of other work spaces (David/Sherry, David/Wayne, David/Anne, Heller/Audrey, Jack/Audrey). Women and children have joined the work force. Most if not all other personal relationships that dare to defy the work sphere are met with death and ruin (Jack/Teri, Jack/Claudia, Wayne/Julia, the Warner family, the Salazars, the Azar family, Edgar's mother, Driscoll's daughter). Again the sweatshop logic permeates everything: if you leave the shop floor *we will hurt you*. Being alive and being on the clock are now essentially synonymous.

Each employee is expected in the normal course of the work day to risk his or her personal well-being. CTU agents can't clock out, but at the same time they are expected to sacrifice life and limb while on the job. Like a sweatshop, where safety guidelines are routinely ignored, the notion of an injury-free work environment is prohibited here. Both Tony and Chase are shot at close range, but then are back working at peek performance within the hour. Jack's heart stops; he is soon back to work. Mason goes terminal with plutonium poisoning, but sticks at his terminal all the way to the grave. Chappelle, Gael, and others all become martyrs to the job.

Forced labor in 24 can be understood, using Marx's terms, via the extension of both absolute and relative surplus: the work day is extended "absolutely" from eight to twenty-four hours, and at the same time the actual minute-by-minute urgency of the work day is elevated "relatively" such that the importance of productivity is measured by the raw horizon of one's own life force.

Informatics as Style

A mathematical detail now rears its head. The chronology lie in 24 is flagrant. Here is a show that not only professes to be concerned with the fidelity of real-time representation – recall Jack's flat voice-over that "events occur in real time" – it goes so far as to avow this commitment, this mathematical obligation, by naming itself after the day-long interval it attempts to document, using the very numerical language of that interval. "Twenty-four." The numbers go like this: minus commercial interruptions, each episode lasts around 42 or 43 minutes; 42 minutes on the hour comes to 70 percent; there are 24 episodes per season; a complete season, therefore, comes to approximately 16.8 hours. So now a second retitling is warranted: not just 24/7 but also 16.8.

Lost forever? Where did all the time go? What happened during those missing moments, those many accumulated interruptions? Of course the obvious answer: commerce happened. But it is more fundamental than that. For, commerce *didn't* happen. It is withheld, both from the perspective of form and narrative. The advertisements are put over "there," while the content is kept over "here." And then later after broadcast, on video for example, the advertisements are excised completely with no explanation at all. This is not to be alarmist, for of course we are dealing here with fictions from the get go, but the fact that the show flaunts its own chronometric failings by denying that they even exist is an indication of a logic of absence and disavowal that is worthy of closer scrutiny. This is the "reality gap" of reality television. There is a chasm, a media hole the length and width of which run thirty percent of the total dimension. What a massive void, all the more awe-inspiring in that it seems not to be missed at all!

Style can be informatic. Narrative and visual style can embody the cultural logic of computation. The "16.8" temporal void reflects itself back on the immediate presence of the whole, as the mode of production becomes synonymous with the show's overall style. In an extension of Raymond Williams' reading of television, we are able to see here the media-formal imprint of capitalist modes of production and distribution on the semiotic logic of the medium. This was already explored above with the discussions around utilitarianism and totality. But it is also evident here, as thirty percent of the material withholds itself, all the while professing its own stopwatch exactitude. It is a classic case of surplus economies and accumulation: the thirty percent void is a surplus and remains hidden, but the surplus always must return in a determining mode to valorize the rest. What a phenomenal rate of return it is.

Each minute, viewed serially one after the next, is of crucial importance. 24 endorses the fantasy that "minutes count," that most people's lives are important on a minute by minute basis. The issue here is not simply the show's central conceit of twenty-four hours making up a single day, for scores of other texts follow this sort of compressed time scenario (from *Ulysses* on down), but that each minute is valuable in succession and only in succession. Thus one must distinguish between the compressed time frame of each "day" and the step by step sequentialism of the day as it unfolds. Because of this the typical film noir formal techniques of flashbacks and ellipses are entirely prohibited in 24, distinguishing it formally from procedurals and cop shows of an earlier time. Following this logic one might mistakenly propose that 24 is, formally speaking, a sort of lowbrow equivalent of Andy Warhol's *Empire* (1964), a film of the Empire State Building that runs continuously for an eight hour fraction of a full day. But again there is an internal "gap" to contend with, for none of the *vérité* chronological signifiers are present in 24: elliptical montage is still used with impunity, there is no interest whatsoever given to ambient or dead time, there are hardly any takes that last longer than several seconds, and so on. Every second is valorized, but only as a hegemonic televisual sign, not as a signifier for a chronology of reality. Hollywood films like *The Set-Up* or *High Noon*, which feature stories transpiring in real time, are much more fitting precursors to the 24 approach.

By giving it the mock title *16.8*, I am proposing that we consider the question of informatics as style. The mathematical precision of it all is what is so fascinating. Why 16.8 hours? Why such a precise number? Why *this* number as opposed to one a little larger or a little smaller? (And what bureau must I petition to recoup my lost time?) The answers are not so clear, but what is indeed clear is the pervasive replacement of one number for another, 24 for 16.8. This is an occult numerology whereby one "special" number is replace by another right at the very moment of its own articulation. The show does *not*

present twenty-four hours to the viewer. So why all this elaborate pretense to suggest otherwise?

Using the concept of "disingenuous informatics," it is possible to see how the show often asserts information as fact,
only to reveal that same information as untrue. One piece of
data, a specific time duration, is swapped for another of lesser
duration but equally as specific. The avowed threat becomes a
spoof. One minute Jack is a traitor, the next minute it was all
an elaborate lie. Every few minutes, the plot of the show flips
radically, as unceasingly as the ticking clock itself. Understand
it as a postfordism of the aesthetic: the audience's immaterial
faculties are elevated over its material ones, as fact and evidence become labile and those formerly stalwart shocker techniques – gore or sex – are neglected as limp and unappetizing.
For every flash of blood there is an equal number of cognitive
tricks and twists. This is pure information as aphrodisiac, a
cult of epistemological reversal. Surprise reversals, the gotcha
ending, thinking one thing and then learning later that it all
was otherwise – these many rapidly unexpected and changing
narrative states evoke an "informatic pleasure" over and above
any sense of visual pleasure. It is Aristotle's peripeteia, only
repeated at such rapid frequency that it eclipses all other
formal techniques. It is informatics as style.

24 blends the many characteristics of the information age
in complicated ways. For example, the body in 24 is construed
not so much as flesh and blood but as an informatic database.
Perhaps the single most emblematic scenario in the show,
the one motif that returns with most regularity and which
sums up the entire signature of 24 in a single gesture, is the
interrogation scene. It is Guantanamo Bay and Abu Ghraib
writ large in the cultural unconscious. But to be clear, interrogation and torture are never questions of punishment in 24.
Torture here is not a question of sadism or wanton violence.
These are never hate crimes. They are never perpetrated out
of bigotry or xenophobia. The 24 interrogation scene always
carries a single goal, *to extract informatic data from organic
bodies.* Interrogation is merely the technique for information
retrieval. The body is a database, torture a query algorithm.
(That such tactics are publicly acknowledged by the CIA and

others to be ineffective at gathering useful data is beside the point; one is dealing here with an entirely fantasmatic logic.) If Jack is impassioned during an interrogation, it is always strictly his own PSYOPS tactic. There is never pleasure-seeking in his sadism. He gets results. It is pure consequentialism, torture as zen.[3]

The 24 interrogation scene privileges information retrieval over all else: the location of a bomb, or the answer to a clue. But it is a question more precisely of information *flows*. Answers are needed back at headquarters, answers that will allow the machines to hone in on the next piece of the puzzle. Bodies inevitably block those flows, contravening a more perfect efficiency of informatic flux. The body in interrogation is never mere flesh, but is an informatic space that must be hacked according to its own proclivities, its own psychological or physiological profile. "Everyone has a breaking point," the viewer is reminded. One must simply hack the particular individual in question according to the precise exploits known to be effective against him and only him. If the body happens to be damaged, as in the case of Paula, the wounded CTU staffer in season two, or the Chinese national in season four, it must be healed just to the point where the corpus is legible again, to proffer a password, to testify, before the body is discarded as no longer informatically viable. Or if a body no longer has any useful information it is summarily executed, as Nina is by Jack in season three. Data equals life. Informatic viability trumps all other considerations, from due process, to mercy, to human rights. In many ways 24 marks a return to the medieval inquisition model of torture. Both exclusively value immaterial rewards, only today it is informatic not spiritual.

Return to the question of informatics as style. Lev Manovich and others have written on the *waning of montage* in the contemporary moving image. It is hard to understate the importance of montage as a twentieth-century cinematic technique. It extends from Lev Kuleshov and Dziga Vertov to the very center of the classic Hollywood continuity method. Montage is as central to the moving image as sound or light. In fact the neglect of montage in the period after the Second World War is often a touchstone for a rejection of hegemonic form in

Figure 4.1. Fox. 24 (Season 5, Episode 21), 2006. Video still.

screen media, as in the long takes of Roberto Rossellini, Frederick Wiseman, Jim Jarmusch, Jean-Luc Godard, or a number of other directors explicitly working outside of the classical Hollywood model, whereas in earlier times, as with Sergei Eisenstein, heightened montage was one of the key ingredients for progressive film form. With the advent of the new media of the late twentieth century it is possible to identify *a waning in the importance and use of montage as a formal technique*, except that today it is not an indicator of any experimental tendency. Manovich notes for example how the aesthetic of "morphing," a technique facilitated by the computer, makes montage no longer central or even necessary, as one image grows and warps into another without a cut or even a dissolve in the cinematic sense.[4] Likewise electronic games, which like the personal computer are also emblematic of the interactive, "new" media, effectively sideline montage as a constitutive formal technique, generally keeping all inter-diegetic action contained within smooth, continuous visual flows and reserving montage for those moments when the user must jump from one gamic layer to another.[5] So the notion of morphing is crucial, but no less important for the waning of montage is the logic of "windowing" whereby more than one image appears framed within the entire screen.[6] This is one of the great aesthetic leaps of the graphical user interface beyond the example set by the cinema: no longer will the viewer experience montage via cuts over time, proceeding from shot to shot, one must now "cut" (but in its opposite, as "suturing") within any given frame, holding two or more source images side by side which themselves will persist montage-free over much longer "takes" than their cinematic predecessors. This phenomena is evident in the windowed personal computer interface, but also in the gaming interface which "windows" using inset, distinct image sources such as the heads-up-display. Fusing cuts within the frame replaces fusing cuts in time.

Undoing chronological montage is one way in which the computer goes beyond cinema. But "beyond" cinema may also indicate a prefiguration of cinema, an undoing of its demands. In 24 the techniques of visual simultaneity follow a priori, historical examples from the visual arts, particularly from certain genres of painting, illustration, and graphic design, whereby multiple panels appear together within a single overall frame, as in a triptych painting, ecclesiastical stained glass, or comic book. (Notably, the polyptych technique in non-digital cinema indicates formal experimentation outside the mainstream, as in the Charles and Ray Eames seven-channel film "Glimpses of the USA" [1959], or any number of multi-channel film or video art installations.) I am speaking now of the technique in 24, and also used with increasing regularity in other television shows and indeed in new film production that has adopted digital editing and postproduction techniques, whereby two or more video clips appear side by side within one frame. It is used at the climax of each episode, as well as going in and out of each commercial break, and additionally throughout the show for special scenarios such as telephone dialogue. The show suggests thus that there is something to be gained aesthetically by seeing more than one discrete perspective at the same time on the screen. This is a formal technique that classical cinema almost never deploys, although with newer digital techniques such conventions have begun to relax. Witness experiments like the recent *Timecode*, which 24 appears to have copied wholesale, or Ang Lee's *Hulk* which remediates comic book panel layouts in a mosaic of multiple images within a single frame.

To formulate a coherent explanation for why this might be the case, return to the question posed at the outset: is this show political? Note that the question is *not*: does the show have a political message? That question is exceedingly more difficult to answer, and is frankly much less interesting. The issue at hand is, rather, the expressive relationship between any given cultural artifact and the larger geopolitical context in which it exists. The question is: is the show, *in itself*, political – not, is it a courier for this or that political ideology. Thus if the viewer can determine the material reality of the current geopolitical context, and interpolate from that a model of semantic expression, as flawed or symptomatic the model might necessarily be, he or she will arrive at a coherent "way of viewing." And this "way" will be political, simply by virtue of it being true.

Having posed the question of the political, a second question becomes crucial: what are the material conditions of contemporary life? Luckily this is not a difficult question to answer, even if the answer is time-consuming in its telling. I will not answer it here in full, only paraphrase the answer by pointing again to Deleuze's concept of the control society: millennial flows of bodies and commodities, the transnationals, flexible accumulation, universal informatic protocols, rhizomatic networks, biomedia, global empire, and so on.

"Flawed or symptomatic" is how I just described the nature of semantic expression. Showing my true colors again, I will side somewhat axiomatically with the Marxian and psychoanalytical notions of semiotic economies. This is a perspective that explains meaning-making and expression through the notion of what Fredric Jameson calls a "political unconscious" wherein cultural production is not simply the act of making a work of art and disseminating it, but instead is understood through complex flows of sublimation, transfer of affect, repression, subject formation, neurosis, and all the other aspects of desiring production. For this we are indebted to a tradition of critical materialism starting with Marx and proceeding through a number of figures including Jacques Lacan and Jameson. The claim that the model is "flawed or symptomatic" is not to discredit its predictive utility, but quite the opposite, to acknowledge the critical gap that must necessarily exist in any theory of mediation. If we are lucky, the act of interpretation itself will realize and confess to the gap, shunning the folly of trying to cleanse the aesthetic by annihilating it in either the utopia of union or the dystopia of exclusion.

Understanding the hermeneutic logic in this way, we can now return to the discussion of visual simultaneity and the waning of montage. Visual simultaneity is indicative of how informatic economies reappear in the show as "style." In other words, what is evident in this show is *the distributed network as an aesthetic construction*, both at the level of narrative and formal design (Fig. 4.1). Since it represents difference through time, traditional montage is less effective at displaying networked relationality. The notion of difference in space is better suited to a single plane which is then bisected one or more times. Hence the polyptych supersedes montage because it is a better representation of informatic networks, perceived as they are as surfaced, flat, horizontal, topological, and synchronic. The "poly-ptych" is, to stress an etymology that Deleuze would have liked, a "multi-fold." It is a single plane that, through its own internal folding, allows multiple significant subsystems to express themselves simultaneously.

Like the "intraface" of Chapter 1, the polyptych is a network that allows for multiple kinds of cross-talk to take place entirely within the interface. But visual simultaneity is also paired with a specific form of narrative construction which likewise privileges the complex synchrony of an ongoing swarm of characters in a web of interaction. This is the visual and narratological equivalent of graph theory and social network theory. Robert Altman is the primary if not first auteur for this technique, aesthetically repurposing in his style the growing importance of interpersonal, "grassroots" networks in the new social movements of the 1970s. Thus, the ambient interconnectedness of story and character in *Nashville* (1975) or later in *Short Cuts* (1993) exists as a sublimation of the growing globalism in which "we're all connected" even if we don't entirely realize how, why, or what for. *Short Cuts* is, in this sense, a friends-of-friends network in which characters are nodes and their various actions and interplays constitute propagating links and gateways to other nodes. (Certainly one might also look earlier to Anthony Mann's lyrical work in *Winchester '73* [1950], a film essentially structured around the networked flows of commodity logistics: one specific commodity, a rifle, gains the status of a character within the film, and the hop-scotch exchange of that commodity through various networked liaisons structures the movement and flow of the narrative overall.) Altman gives some historical context, then, to the growing emphasis today on serendipity and concurrency in narrative media (not to mention the use of ensemble casts rather than single lead actors): two things happening to happen in the same time or place, which may or may not overlap or "link." Today the Altman touch has gone mainstream, essentially becoming a new dominant, as seen in millennial films like *Babel* (2006), *Code Unknown* (2000), *Crash* (2004), *Magnolia* (1999), *Syriana* (2005) or *Traffic* (2000), all of which devolve into a narrative construction of pure rhizomatic imbrication. In these films a number of relatively autonomous, yet ultimately interconnected, subnarratives proceed in parallel, often interconnecting for logical reasons or for reasons of happenstance. The thick latticework of relationships is of course not without precedent. *24*'s iteration owes as much to the soap opera as it does to Altman or Paul Thomas Anderson. And in the 1990s directors like Quentin Tarantino and Krzysztof Kieslowski paved the way for the millennial films. Regardless, this unique brand of narrative and visual simultaneity is one of the newly identifiable formal techniques in the control society.

Lost in the serendipity of interconnection, these films also ground themselves in moments of totality, those extraordinary events that unite the entire network under a global-single entrainment. This too is *binary*: either the social network is a raw assemblage of entirely uncoupled and discontinuous mini worlds, or through a phase shift the network unifies into a single presence. The network forces a logic of binary decision: either a flood, or an idle connection; either pandemic or standby mode. In *Magnolia* the totalizing event is a song sung in unison followed by a plague of frogs that unites globally, across space and subnet; in *Short Cuts* it is an earthquake that cuts an orthogonal swath across all stories and characters (contrast this to the similar earthquake in the end of *San Francisco* [1936] which is a vehicle for the massification of humanity during an early moment in modernity, rather than its disparate interconnectedness in today's information age). In 24 the global-single event is expressed most clearly in the nuclear bomb explosion in season two, but each season has its singular exceptional event, whether it be an assassination attempt, the infection of patient zero, or something else. Every far-flung story line pauses during these special moments, and across the entire network a singular focus emerges.

Yielding to these many details, we should agree that 24 is a political show, but perhaps for entirely different reasons than might have been assumed as the outset. We should shy away from the simplistic cause-and-effect model that points to the Fox network as an ideological institution, or to various utilitarian claims made by the show's characters, extrapolating from these many overt "content analyses" toward some overarching political message. Instead, 24 is political because the show embodies in its formal technique the essential grammar of the control society, dominated as it is by specific network and informatic logics.

Specific socio-historical realities will emerge in the reading of any cultural artifact. The subject's responsibility is to identify expressive connections between the formal construction of the medium and the socio-historical realities in which it is embedded. These expressive connections are never neat and tidy, of course, but that is precisely what makes the act of interpretation so fun to begin with.

Overall, what is the ideology of the aesthetic? It is an historical and material productive circuit which both prescribes, in a stochastic if not outright manner, the formal grammar of any given aesthetic medium, yet nevertheless is the retroactive effect of that very grammar accumulated over time and culture.

Postscript: We Are the Gold Farmers

"Do we really need another analysis of how a cultural representation does symbolic violence to a marginal group?" This is how one colleague recently put it, suggesting that the cultural studies and identity politics movements of the 1980s and 1990s had at last exhausted their utility.

But how could an ostensibly liberal, broad-minded person say such a thing? How did we get here? How did the world slip away from the 1960s mold, in which the liberation of desire (and thus affective identities of various kinds) was considered a politically progressive project to undertake? At the turn of the new millennium a different destiny lies ahead. Today, under the new postfordist economies, desire and identity are part of the core economic base and thus woven into the value chain more than ever before.[1] What cruelty of fate. If marginal groups are now "normalized" within the mode of production, what would it mean to offer criticism of the present situation? Is there any outside anymore, when networks encircle the globe? Any subaltern, when all are tethered to the communications apparatus?

This book has tried to address some of these questions by showing how digital aesthetics both prohibit and facilitate political encounters. At the outset I suggested that we think of media not so much as objects but as principles of mediation. In this sense, the computer should be understood as an ethic or a practice, in that it introduces a structure of action, a recipe for moving procedurally toward a certain state of affairs. The primary site for such investigations has been the interface, since it is the point of transition from one entity to another. Yet, countering the received assumptions that interfaces are doors or windows, connecting things to other things, I tried to argue in Chapters 1 and 2 that the digital interface in fact produces an autonomous zone of interaction, orthogonal to the human sensorium, concerned as much with unworkability and obfuscation as with connectivity and transparency. Faced with the breakdown of the interface, it was necessary, in Chapters 3 and 4, to interrogate representability as such. Can media artifacts depict control society, and if so, how? To end I will consider one final interface, the human interface itself, and then offer some concluding meditations on the virtues of generic personhood in the age of the control society.

A specter haunts the world of digital games, the specter of the "Chinese gold farmer." But who is this shadowy figure? The Chinese gold farmer is a gamer who plays online video games day and night in order to earn virtual gold and sell it for real money. Journalists and researchers have stalked this elusive pirate around the world, uncovering computer rooms in China stocked with young gamers toiling in meager conditions for inferior pay.[2]

But is it as simple as all that? Such narratives are often accepted at face value, without probing more deeply into the powerful repercussions of the stereotypes they contain. I want to suggest that the specter of the Chinese gold farmer is in fact performing powerful ideological work within contemporary culture. The gold farmer is an allegorical portrait for how identity exists online, a portrait not so much of the orientalized other, but of ourselves.

To triangulate this state of affairs, the chapter will unfold around four queries. The first is an inquiry into the contemporary status of race, in parallel with a few observations about the state of cultural theory. The second and third questions deal directly with representations of race in video games and elsewhere. And the final question offers something of a suggestion, a possible reassessment of the situation itself, not so much a "way out" of the problems presented here, but an alternate beginning that shows, if it is successful, how some of the problems might not actually be problems in the first place, provided one is willing to leave them be.

First Question: *Ubinam Gentium Sumus?* Or, Where in the World Are We?

How did we get here? Step back and recall two larger points of socio-historical context informing the present debate. The first concerns the question of how race is represented today in culture, and the second concerns the so-called failure of theory and the turn, in recent years, away from identity politics and cultural criticism.

For the first point of context, recall the inauguration of the American President Barack Obama in January 2009 – not the ceremony itself, but the rehearsal that took place just prior to the event (Fig. 5.1). Three figures appear on the platform, the

Figure 5.1. Stand-ins for President-elect Barack Obama, his wife Michelle Obama, and Chief Justice John Roberts rehearse the swearing-in ceremony for the inauguration on the West Front of the US Capitol, Monday, January 19, 2009 in Washington, DC (AP/World Wide Photos, used with permission.)

same three who would be present during the swearing in. Barack Obama's stand-in is a black man, Michelle Obama's a black woman, and Justice John Roberts' a white man.

Who are these people? Who orchestrated this event? One may assume that the stand-ins for this rehearsal are drawn from the White House aide corps or perhaps from the Secret Service, their roles in the rehearsal being merely to stand in certain places and follow the choreography of simple sequences of events. Yet the specificity of the roles is particularly interesting: this black man for that black man, this black woman for that black woman, this white man for that white man. Why go to such lengths to enforce such racial specificity body by body? The casting of these particular three stand-ins might not mean much at all. Indeed a number of practical concerns most likely influenced the decision, practical concerns such as lighting and camera placement.

Even then, is there not evidence here, in Obama's inauguration rehearsal, of the most idealized form of racial typing? After Obama's election many began to speak of a post-racial society. But focus on the inauguration rehearsal. Even during this rehearsal, even during a moment in which race no longer matters, it appears to matter more than anything else. In the most prosaic dress rehearsal of who steps when and where, of moving television cameras around, of determining the temporal sequences of events – at this very moment of absolute banality, the logic of race nevertheless holds sway, all the more aggressive by virtue of its very innocuousness.

Consider for a moment the logic of superstition. "Of course *I'm* not superstitious," the level-headed person says. "I know that it doesn't *really* matter if I step on a crack, or walk under a ladder, or place a hat on a bed." Occult ritual – doing one thing to ward off another – has *nothing* to do with how the world really works. Common knowledge, claims the level-headed person. Yet it is precisely in such moments of "common knowledge" that the logic of superstition intervenes. Precisely because it doesn't matter where one places a hat, all the more reason to adhere militantly to the rules of correct behavior. The fact that the decision is free makes it all the more necessary to choose correctly. It is absolutely meaningless, so why risk it. Why walk under a ladder rather than not, when the two paths are equivalent and one may just as easily avoid it?

Such is the logic of race in the Obama inauguration rehearsal: *of course race doesn't matter, which is why it must be preserved at all cost.* The open societies of global neoliberalism have reached a state in which race matters absolutely, but only because it does not matter at all any more. The very lack of necessity drills forward like an irresistible force. Thus racial coding has not so much disappeared in recent years, but rather simply migrated into the realm of dress rehearsal, the realm of the ideal, the realm of pure simulation, and as simulation it remains absolutely necessary. The Obama body doubles, as pure simulation, *must be black.*

Perhaps this indicates the next phase in racial representation. After Jim Crow, after civil rights, race today has been liberated, but only so it may persist in a purely simulated form (and in its being simulated it finds a natural home in the digital). With the media of simulation we have entered the phase of purely idealized racial coding, no longer merely the dirty racism of actual struggle. Now after the "formal" subsumption of racial logic comes the "real" subsumption. With Obama racial typing is finally liberated so that it may exist in a purely ideological form. In essence, the most perfect racial typing is that which lives inside a mediated simulation.

The reason for this is that the virtual can *only* exist within the absolute; the virtual *needs* the absolute. Yet conventional wisdom often suggests the reverse, that the virtual is the thing that stands "above" or apart from the real, that all anxieties about the real ultimately find their escape in the virtual. But here the conventional wisdom is wrong, for the exact opposite is true. The virtual can only be possible, not in relation to the real, but in relation to the absolute.

In formalizing this slightly, the following two points emerge: (1) the absolute realm of mediatic simulation is responsible for the "perfection" (i.e. "completion" or "accomplishment") of racial typing, and that (2) the virtual is responsible for projecting race forward into mediatic simulation, or in other words, for pushing race into the enterprise of value creation.

I will advance to the question of how race enters the sphere of value creation in a moment. First let me examine more closely the present social and historical context, particularly the so-called failure of theory, and the turn, in recent years, away from identity politics and cultural criticism.[3]

Consider again the lament cited at the top of the chapter. "Do we really need another analysis of how a cultural representation does symbolic violence to a marginal group?" Instead of passing this off as merely the insensitivity of a white liberal academic turning a blind eye to matters of racial and cultural injustice, it is important to point out a far more fundamental trend that is at work here. For in certain philosophical circles there exists today a newfound desire to divorce politics from ontology. There exists a desire to neuter the force of critique by removing dialectical reason from the structure of being. As this particular individual put it, the terms of the new philosophy will be: "a rejection of textual analysis or linguistic structures, a positive ontology and desire to attain the Absolute, and an attempt to shed all anthropocentrism." But what does this mean? The first term, a rejection of textual analysis, refers to literary criticism and the perception that textual approaches gained too much ground particularly in the decades following the 1960s, so much so that they must be curtailed in favor of realist or non-interpretive approaches. The second term, a positive ontology, refers (as best one can surmise) to the "affirmative" ontology of someone like Deleuze, who removes the dialectical negative entirely from his theory of being. While the third term, the shedding of all anthropocentrism, refers to a demotion of the human, such that mankind is on an equal footing with all other objects in the world, no more privileged and no less privileged than other kinds of entities.

Is it a surprise that the identity politics and cultural theory movements have experienced such a crisis of faith? Even the most hardline defenders of leftist theory admit the same thing, that no one really believes in postmodernism any more. Even Jameson, in his *A Singular Modernity*, put forward a new take on the postmodern as something of an echo of the modern, something to be folded back, something to be reversed and reincorporated into a singular periodization. It was easy to sneer at those who slowed the march of civil rights, or cluck at a politically incorrect remark. But perhaps a total reversal has taken place without anyone knowing. Perhaps the bottom has fallen out. Perhaps we are all Alan Sokal now.

But is it any surprise that, just at the moment when identity and affect become incorporated into the digital markets of postfordism, the utility of identity and affect as critical categories comes into question? Shall we not discard our discussions of affective "faciality" in favor of a new defacement? Recall Tiqqun's diagnosis of the present political landscape of empire, that "Empire does not confront us like a subject, facing us, but like an *environment* that is hostile to us."[4] Is the sixties-era liberation of affect really a new kind of obscenity, a new pornography in which all must be exposed for speculation and investment?

Michael Hardt and Antonio Negri fired one of the first volleys in this new skirmish over the utility of certain critical tactics, specifically the elevation of multiple affects and subjectivities by those working within leftist cultural theory:

> We suspect that postmodernist and postcolonialist theories may end up in a dead end because they fail to recognize adequately the contemporary object of critique, that is, they mistake today's real enemy. What if the modern form of power these critics (and we ourselves) have taken such pains to describe and contest no longer holds sway in our society? What if these theorists are so intent on combating the remnants of a past form of domination that they fail to recognize the new form that is looming over them in the present? What if the dominating powers that are the intended object of critique have mutated in such a way as to depotentialize any such postmodernist challenge? In short, what if a new paradigm of power, a postmodern sovereignty, has come to replace the modern paradigm and *rule through differential hierarchies of the hybrid and fragmentary subjectivities* that these theorists celebrate? In this case, modern forms of sovereignty would no longer be at issue, and the postmodernist and postcolonialist strategies that appear to be liberatory would not challenge but in fact coincide with and even unwittingly reinforce the new strategies of rule! . . . This new enemy not only is resistant to the old weapons but actually thrives on them, and thus joins its would-be

antagonists in applying them to the fullest. Long live difference!
Down with essentialist binaries![5]

As might be expected Hardt and Negri were met by a consid-
erable amount of resistance for taking this position, particularly from those scandalized by the notion that postmodernist
theories about cultural identity might not be as effective as
once thought, and may even add fuel to systems of power and
domination. But Hardt and Negri were not speaking alone;
other voices soon added themselves to the chorus. Both Alain
Badiou and Slavoj Žižek, for example, have made it clear that
they oppose so-called postmodern theory and the fragmentary
subjectivities and liberated affects that supposedly go along
with it. With his book *In Defense of Lost Causes* Žižek advocates
a return to universal truth, leftist theory's erstwhile enemy,
and thus an end to postmodernism's skepticism toward "grand
narratives," a skepticism which he rightly associates with the
corrosive properties of capitalism.[6] Badiou goes even further,
staking much of his work on a theory of the subject bound not
by "fragmentary subjectivities" but grounded in the universality of truth. This newfound interest in a singular, universal
truth is also shared by Susan Buck-Morss in her recent *Hegel,
Haiti, and Universal History*:

> Can we rest satisfied with the call for acknowledging "multiple
> modernities," with a politics of "diversality," or "multiversality,"
> when in fact the inhumanities of these multiplicities are often
> strikingly the same? Critical theoretical practice today is caught
> within the prisonhouse of its own academic debates. . . We exist
> behind cultural borders, the defense of which is a boon to politi-
> cians. The fight to free the facts from the collective histories in
> which they are embedded is one with exposing and expanding the
> porosity of a global social field, where individual experience is not
> so much hybrid as human. . . It is not that truth is multiple or
> that the truth is a whole ensemble of collective identities with
> partial perspectives. Truth is singular, but it is a continuous
> process of inquiry because it builds on a present that is moving
> ground. History keeps running away from us, going places we,
> mere humans, cannot predict. The politics of scholarship that I
> am suggesting is neutrality, but not of the nonpartisan, "truth lies

in the middle" sort; rather, it is a *radical* neutrality that insists on the porosity of the space between enemy sides, a space contested and precarious, to be sure, but free enough for the idea of humanity to remain in view.[7]

Truth is thus singular, Buck-Morss suggests, and achieved through a "radical neutrality" of the human. (A point I will return to at the end.)

But perhaps the most forceful push away from subject-oriented, relativistic, and correlationist thinking has come from Quentin Meillassoux, in his *After Finitude*. Through a highly technical intervention, Meillassoux rejects the hegemony of finitude and urges us to awake from our slumber and reconcile ourselves with the absolute.[8]

Citing these different authors exposes a trend, and accentuates the contrast between a dawning set of concerns and those of the immediate past. Consider for example Gayatri Chakravorty Spivak's much cited essay "Can the Subaltern Speak?,"[9] an article that helped set the stakes for a whole field of critical race theory, particularly in the area of postcolonialism. Spivak's "subaltern" refers not simply to the historically disenfranchised. Subaltern is not simply the subordinate position within any given structural relationship, such as that of Woman, Proletarian, or Gay. There is another level of remove. The subaltern is that quasi-subject structured as Other through a relationship of difference vis-à-vis imperial power. The subaltern is precisely the one who does not have a seat at the table. It is the one who can not petition the powers-that-be, the one who is not – or is not yet – a wage slave for capital.

If Spivak's "can the subaltern speak?" is emblematic of the 1980s and 1990s period of cultural politics, today the very terms of the question have changed dramatically. The question today is not so much *can* the subaltern speak, for the new global networks of technicity have solved this problem with ruthless precision, but *where* and *how* the subaltern speaks, or indeed *is forced* to speak. It is not so much a question of *can* but *does*, not so much a politics of exclusion as a politics of subsumption. (And to be clear: "speech" means something entirely different under this new regime.) The crucial political question is now therefore not so much that of the liberation of affect, as it was for our forebears in the civil rights movement, the gay liberation movement, or the women's movement, in which the elevation of new subject positions, from out of the shadows of oppression, was paramount. The crucial question now is – somehow – the reverse. Not exactly the repression of affect, but perhaps something close. Perhaps something like a politics of subtraction or a politics of disappearance. Perhaps the true digital politics of race, then, would require us not to "let it be," but *leave it be*. Something else is necessary, a *something* of the political. In short, Obama's body double should not necessarily have to be black. It should be whatever it is.

So where in the world are we?[10] To summarize the sociohistorical context: (1) there comes an increased cultivation of racial typing and a triumph of the decades-long quest to liberate affect, concurrent with (2) the recession of "theory," particularly identity politics and cultural theory. At first glance these two phenomena might appear unconnected. They might appear as merely contradictory effects, pushing each other apart, tied together only by historical coincidence. It is thus necessary to pose the question explicitly: Are these two forces connected? And the answer is most certainly yes.

Second Question: Why Do Games Have Races and Classes?

The Obama inauguration rehearsal is not informatic per se, beyond the admittedly vague references given already to simulation and the virtual. To pull back the curtain a bit, consider now cultural production and the digital infrastructure, particularly video games and the kinds of worlds they create. A curious logic holds sway in these digital realms. A curious logic of race and class, constructed via complex software algorithms, still grips the psyche of game makers and game players. But why?

In a game, a race designates a set of representational proclivities – across both diegetic and nondiegetic representation – that are closely followed in matters of narrative, character modeling and animation, gamic elements such as weapons and resources, *mise en scène*, algorithmic personalities, styles of gameplay, AI behaviors, and so on. These types of software artifacts are then "metaphorically patched"[11] into games as coherent, contained "races."

Gamic races are often essentialist in nature, paralleling certain offline retrograde notions of naturally or physiologically determined and unchangeable human races. For example in a game like *World of Warcraft* race is conditioned largely by the demands of aesthetic representation of certain "ethnic" intangibles like voice, visage, and so on, and only secondarily intersects with informatic modeling of behavior in so-called racial traits. For example the troll race in *World of Warcraft* (Fig. 5.2) speaks with a Jamaican accent. Yet in a game like *StarCraft* race is much more algorithmically foundational. In

Figure 5.2. Troll race. Blizzard Entertainment. *World of Warcraft*, 2004. Game still.

StarCraft, a race has unique combat strategies, a certain "way of doing things." To be sure, "race" here pertains to an entirely gamic context, a context which is altogether different from but in some senses determined by offline race. Yet in this sense *StarCraft* is more sinister in that it provides a direct mapping of race onto machinic variables, whereas *World of Warcraft* offloads almost all of this functionality to the sister concept, class, retaining race largely for the window dressing of diegetic representation.

After these software clusters are metaphorically patched into the game as distinct races, the game designers seek balance in gameplay by fine tuning different variables within each software cluster, reducing a value in one faction and augmenting it in an oppositional faction. In this way, all the races are brought into balance. For example, if one *StarCraft* race is inordinately powerful certain racial variables may be quantitatively increased or decreased. The goal is to create a better sense of equilibrium in play. Since each software cluster is apt to be quite complex, the techniques of racial balancing generally operate in a rather roundabout way, eschewing any neat and tidy trade-off between this or that trait mirrored across two or more races. Instead, balance is achieved through the delicate art of exchanging qualitatively different values, for example by shaving *time* off one racial ability and transmuting it into a *damage* boost in another race's ability. If the simulated system involves three races as in *StarCraft*, or an even larger number of classes as in *World of Warcraft*, the art of balance can be exceedingly difficult, ultimately measurable in certain global statistics such as win-loss percentages for each race, or that intangible statistic known elusively as fun.

Certainly much more could be said here about races and classes in games, and the distinction between them, but one particular observation is necessary before moving on, that these games subscribe to a specific notion of race and class (and one not dissimilar to the offline): *race is static and universal, while class is variable and learned.* So in *World of Warcraft* racial traits indeed exist and have a bearing on gameplay, but they are unmodifiable (alas, the troll-Jamaican alliance is incorruptible), while class traits are configurable in a number of significant ways including the talent tree and the boosting of class abilities via consumables or wearables. What this means is that race is "unplayable" in any conventional sense, for all the tangible details of gamic race (voice, visage, character animation, racial abilities, etc.) are quarantined into certain hardcoded machinic behaviors, what I have elsewhere called the "diegetic machine act."[12] One cannot "play" race in *World of Warcraft*. One must accept it as such. Certainly the enterprising gamer can "play with" race via the chat channel, fan comics, and so on. But to *play* with race and to play *with* race are two entirely different things.

The worrisome conclusion is that this view on digital race is typically what one would call, in the offline context, racism, in that the apparatus assigns from without certain identifiable traits to distinct classes of entities and then builds complex machineries for explaining and maintaining the natural imperviousness of it all. That the game pleads innocence by placing the narrative in a fantasy world of fantasy races (trolls, gnomes, elves) does not absolve it from foregrounding a systemic, "cybertype"[13] logic of naturalized group definition and division, as in a dream when the most important or traumatic details are paraded before the mind's eye in such flagrant obviousness that one is blind to them in their very immediacy. The "innocence" of the sublimation is in fact apropos because it illustrates the neoliberal, digirati notion that race must be liberated via an uncoupling from material detail, but also that the logic of race can never be more alive, can never be more *purely* actualized, than in a computer simulation. Apparently one must leave this world in order to actualize more fully its mechanisms of management and discipline.

Let it be underscored though that the most interesting thing to observe here is *not* that *World of Warcraft* is racist. The interesting thing to observe is precisely the way in which racial coding must always pass into fantasy before it can ever return to the real. The true is only created by way of an extended detour through falsity.

But is gaming's race problem merely a nominal one? Is "race" simply an unfortunate word choice for what is ultimately a pragmatic design requirement, that many games require clusters of algorithmic representational proclivities to designate distinct players and player types. If game designers had used a different word like "archetype," "species," or "family" would the problem go away? The answer lies certainly in the deployment of what Lisa Nakamura calls "menu-driven identities" – with or without reference to race – but also in the disheartening discovery that ethnic and racial coding seem always to be synonymous with mediation itself.[14] The one implies the other. By way of an allusion to the *Star Wars* movies, this is what might be called the "Jar Jar Binks" problem of fantasy representation (Fig. 5.3): the more one seems to extricate oneself from the mire of terrestrial stereotyping, the more free and flexible the bigotry machine becomes, able to repopulate the racialized imagination with "aliens," but aliens that conveniently still stick to the gangly comic relief of the blackface minstrel complete with exaggerated facial features and a Jamaican accent. (Jar Jar Binks borrows the voice, but not the body, of black actor Ahmed Best.) Similar scenarios occur in any number of other digital animations, as in the 2001 animated feature *Shrek* where black actor Eddie Murphy quite literally plays the ass. Apparently computers are much better at this than we could ever have imagined! Because of this, the contemporary format of digital animation, both cinematic and gamic, is one of the most important sites today where racial coding is worked out in mass culture. Until this issue is addressed, the "race" problematic in gaming will be alive and well, no matter what name it goes by.[15]

Third Question: Who Is the Chinese Gold Farmer?

But what of the market system in general, where does it appear? Markets are places where the standardized exchange of qualitatively different entities takes place in a naturalized, unfettered fashion following certain ground rules. Most all games are markets of some form or another. RTS games in particular – races and all – simulate markets quite vividly with their economics of resource collection and exchange. To be sure this is entirely different from the claim, issuing from

Figure 5.3. Jar Jar Binks publicity image for *Star Wars, Episodes I-III* (d. George Lucas, 1999–2005).

certain economists, that games like *Everquest* or *World of Warcraft* are markets due to the circulation of virtual gold within them.[16] Rather, this is the claim that RTS games (a genre shared not by *World of Warcraft* but by its predecessor *Warcraft III* as well as *StarCraft*) are markets because the algorithms of gameplay themselves are structured around an economy of resources and productive capabilities. Resources circulate, objects and agents are produced, destroyed and replenished, all without the exchange of "gold" or the existence of virtual "marketplaces" in any proper sense. The market analogy is significant because it highlights the problem of how to "control" that which is uncontrollable, or how to shift from top-down control to organic, bottom-up control.

The specter of the Chinese gold farmer returns again now as a way of addressing the question of markets in games. Recall the narrative again, that somewhere off in another land beyond the sea there are legions of Chinese gamers, working in near sweatshop conditions, playing games to earn real cash for virtual objects. I have no interest in disputing this on purely empirical grounds. Of course such rooms exist, here, there, and elsewhere. But of much greater importance, it seems, is the ideological work being performed by the tableau itself: "the problem of the Chinese gold farmer." A certain amount of ideological demystification is in order, if not to shrug off the xenophobia latent in such a formulation, then to invert the terms entirely.

What if something else is happening? What if the "problem of the Chinese gold farmer" is really a decoy for what is actually going on? In order to tackle the problem directly, consider the first of two affirmations: (1) *We are the gold farmers.* (And by "we" I mean the gamers and users of the developed and developing worlds alike, the unified mass of whites and non-whites alike.)

What does this mean, that *we are the gold farmers?* It means that in the age of postfordist capitalism it is impossible to differentiate cleanly between play and work. It is impossible to differentiate cleanly between nonproductive leisure activity existing within the sphere of play and productive activity existing within the sphere of the workplace. Such a claim should be understood both in a general and specific sense. In general, postfordist workspaces are those that have ballooned outward into daily life to such a high degree that labor is performed via phone in the car, on email walking down the street, or at home after putting the children to bed. Crosscutting this outward expansion is an internal collapse of the workspace itself, as the "bored at work" classes invent new ways to slack off on the job, surfing the web, and otherwise circumventing the necessities of workplace always-on performance. But also in a more specific sense, postfordism is a mode of production that makes life itself the site of valorization, that is to say, it turns seemingly normal human behavior into monetizable labor. The new consumer titans Google or Amazon are the masters in this domain. No longer simply a blogger, someone performs the necessary labor of knitting networks together. No longer simply a consumer, browsing through links on an e-commerce site, someone is offloading his or her tastes and proclivities into a data-mining database with each click and scroll. No longer simply keeping up with email correspondence, someone is presiding over the creation and maintenance of codified social relationships. Each and every day, anyone plugged into a network is performing hour after hour of unpaid micro labor. In this sense are we not gold farmers too? Why are our dreary hours spent in front of the screen any different? We troll and scroll, tagging and clicking, uploading and contributing, posting and commenting. They spider us and mine us, extracting value from pure information. Our drudgery is rewarded from time to time of course, with bribes of free this and free that, a free email account or a free ringtone. I do not dispute the existence of a business plan. Rather I dispute the ideological mystification that says that we are the free while the Chinese children are in chains, that our computers are a lifeline and their computers are a curse. This kind of obscenity must be thrown out. We are all gold farmers, and all the more paradoxical since most of us do it willingly and for no money at all.

Now a second affirmation: (2) *It's not the gold, it's the Chinese.* In order to understand further the kind of ideological force behind the so-called problem of the Chinese gold farmer, one must acknowledge that it is not the gold that is being farmed, it is the "Chinese" that is being farmed. The purely economic claim from the first affirmation must now be supplemented. As has been hinted thus far, there is a new kind of speech online, the speech of the body, the codified value it produces when it is captured, massified, and scanned by systems of monetization. The purely economic claim, then, that all users perform scads of unpaid micro labor, merely through the act of living inside the digital cocoon, must be supplemented via an examination of the very quality of that act. So the hunter becomes the hunted, migrating from a situation in which users farm for gold, to a situation in which users are being farmed. For, under postfordism, the act of life is always already an act of affective identity. A body is always "cybertyped," that is to say, it is always tagged with a certain set of affective identity markers. Whenever a body speaks, it always already speaks as a body codified with an affective identity (gendered, ethnically typed, and so on), determined as such by various infrastructures both of and for identity formation. The difficulty is not simply that bodies must always speak. The difficulty is that they must always speak *as*.

Let there be no misunderstanding, my goal is not the elimination of difference, racial or otherwise. Rather what must be interrogated is, on the one hand, when difference becomes fodder for injustice, and on the other hand, when difference is mobilized as fuel for value creation in the marketplace. The goal, then, would be to uncouple difference from both injustice and valorization.

With the postfordist colonization of affect and the concomitant valorization of affective difference, a body has no choice but to speak. A body speaks whether it wants to or not. This is the genius of the "page rank" algorithm used by search engines: use graph theory to valorize pure heterogenity, show how quality is an emergent property of quantity, as Barbara Cassin has written in her book on Google.[7] Data mining is often considered in terms of location and extraction of nuggets of information from a sea of background noise. But this metaphor is entirely wrong. Data mining is essentially a plastic art, for it responds to the sculpture of the medium itself, to the background noise itself. It valorizes the pure shape of relationships. Not "can" but "does" the body speak? Yes, it has no choice.

Making a phone call from the slums of Cairo or Mumbai or Paris, the subaltern "speaks" into a database – just as much as I do when I pick up the phone. The difference for difference is no longer actual, it is technical. The subaltern speaks, and somewhere an algorithm listens.

Final Question: Does the Whatever Speak?

At the very moment of the digital, at the very moment of the prohibition of the negative, from out of the trenches of forced speech, of enforced behavior, of networks reinforced with apparatuses of capture and protocols for ebb and flow, here rises a new politics of disappearance. It is no longer the Hegel of history, where everything is "post-" this and "post-" that, but the Hegel of the negative, where everything is "un-" or "non-" What was once a logic of supercession is now a logic of cancellation. Seek not the posthuman, but the nonhuman. Be not post identity, but rather subtractive of it. The operative political question today, thus, in the shadow of digital markets, is not that of confrontation on equal footing, not "what are they going to do to us?" or even "what are we going to do to them?," but rather the exodus question: first posed as "what are we going to do *without* them?" and later posed in a more sophisticated sense as "what are we going to do without *ourselves*?" Cease trying to buttress presence with new predicates, it is time now to abandon it, to leave it be. It is time now for leaving-being.

The virtual (or the new, the *next*) is no longer the site of emancipation. Rather, it is the primary mechanism of oppression. And so, even in the face of those who seek alternatives to this world of debasement and exploitation, we must stress that it is not the job of politics to invent a new world. On the contrary it is the job of politics to make all these new worlds irrelevant. No politics can be derived today from a theory of the new.[18] The reason is simple: we have never known any form of modernity except that form of modernity subservient to the new. We have never known any form of modernity except that of market accumulation, increased profit margins, development of the productive forces, rises in productivity, new jingles, the latest fads, and on and on. These are the currency of the realm. It is time now to subtract from this world, not add to it. The challenge today is not one of political or moral imagination, for this problem was solved ages ago – kill the despots, surpass capitalism, inclusion of the excluded, equality for all of humanity, end exploitation. The world does not need new ideas. The challenge is simply to realize what we already know to be true.

That silly slogan of the left, "another world is possible," should be scrapped. Another world is not possible. The political is that thing that can not happen. It can not be produced and it can not take place. But why? Because "production" and "taking place" are the domain of anti-political forces. The political does not arise from the domain of production, nor does it exist in any place or situation. Another vocabulary is required. So like Badiou we might speak of the political in terms of the event. Or like Laruelle we might speak in terms of generic immanence.

The "me" today is the *whatever*. Recall Buck-Morss' concept of a "singular" truth reached via "radical neutrality." Or recall what Rey Chow once described as the "indifference" of the native.[19] These are hints into the meaning of this elusive concept. But what exactly is the whatever? Now the question may be answered more fully.

The concept of the whatever comes from the writing of a number of different authors, all working roughly in the terrain of continental philosophy and political theory. While the concept has roots in the scholastics and can be found in thinkers as divergent as Pierce, Levinas, and Lyotard, the whatever gained traction in the current discourse largely because of Deleuze and then later via more sustained considerations by Agamben. Deleuze uses the concept of the "whatever" and the "any-space-whatever" in his *Cinema* books, and deploys related terminology in other texts, such as the "something" (*aliquid*) and the "neutral" in *Logic of Sense*, and "haecceity" (the Latinate term borrowed from Duns Scotus meaning "thisness") in *A Thousand Plateaus*. In *The Coming Community* Agamben explains his use of the term in greater detail: "The Whatever in question here relates to singularity not in its indifference with respect to a common property (to a concept, for example: being red, being French, being Muslim), but only in its being *such as it is*."[20] And later: "Whatever is the figure of pure singularity. Whatever singularity has no identity, it is not determinate with respect to a concept, but neither is it simply indeterminate; rather it is determined only through its relation to an *idea*, that is, to the totality of its possibilities."[21] The whatever follows a logic of belonging (*x* such that it belongs to *y*), not a logic of predication (*x* is defined through *y*, or more simply, *x* is *y*).[22]

The trick of the whatever is thus to abstain from the assignation of traits, to abstain from the system of biopolitical predication, to abstain from the bagging and tagging of bodies.[23] This does not mean that all bodies are now blank. Quite the opposite. All bodies are full. But their fullness is a generic fullness, a fullness of whatsoever they are.[24] Likewise it does not mean that difference has "gone away." The opposite is the case, as difference may now finally come into its own as generic difference.

The whatever is often confused with two other kinds of subjects that, while similar, are ultimately incompatible. The first is the postfordist economic subject. It would be a mistake to think that the whatever is merely the fully unique, customized, qualitatively special postfordist consumer – what Tiqqun calls "Bloom," the subject for whom everything is tailored and targeted.[25] For each affective predilection of the postfordist economic subject there is a corresponding marketplace that will satisfy it. Here lies the Pyrrhic victories of identity politics: each woman a woman consumer, each black a black consumer, each gay a gay consumer, each chicano a chicano consumer. For in our delivery from oppression, were we not also delivered to a new site of consumption? This was precisely the point made previously about the Chinese gold farmer: every economic transaction today is also an affective transaction (which is to say a transaction that will likely deal with aspects such as, but not limited to, racial identity).

Second is the liberal political subject. It would also be a mistake to think that the whatever is akin to something like the "original position" and "veil of ignorance" described by John Rawls in his theory of justice, but evident as well in other forms across a number of different liberal social theories. The veil-of-ignorance subject must hold in suspension its gender, its ethnicity, its religious affiliation, its class position, etc. In the digital context it is often summed up by the slogan "on the Internet nobody knows your identity." (A position that was once famously parodied as "on the Internet nobody knows you're a dog.") The Rawlsian liberal fantasy is thus that of the transcendental subject par excellence, the subject who is able to step out of his skin, suspending social relations in order to observe them from a position of supposed neutrality. (The dilemma with Rawls is that some models of social relations are *not* suspended, specifically those borrowed from liberal political economy and game theory: respect for individual liberty, the maximization of advantage, rational choice, and so on. Again the demon of simulation rears its head, as things appear neutral precisely at the point of *least* neutrality.) Given this characterization of the liberal political subject it would be a mistake to think that it has much at all in common with the whatever.

Remember that, after the old enemy of transcendental essentialism, racial justice has a new enemy, transient anti-essentialism. Recall the conceit of white privilege: to cast off the fetters of race and retreat to the original position behind a veil of ignorance (as in Rawls). Such a theory reveals not only the ignorance of the veil, but also the ignorance of the position, for it is only certain select bodies, certain select subjects, who are free to cast off their earthly fetters and go blank, like a white sheet of paper.

What of those bodies of color for whom this is not an option? Or what about those who simply have no desire to abandon themselves, to abandon their culture, to abandon their history? For whom would this be called justice? What even of those bona fide whatever bodies who nevertheless are constructed and viewed as such from the perspective of the dominant? Did they bring it upon themselves? Do they wish it to be so? Clearly such subaltern positions exist entirely within normative discursive structures.

The rebuttal from the whatever is: yes, the old system of transcendental essentialism is still our enemy, we do not want to return to a politics of essential purity in which only certain subjects are dominant and all others are consigned to alterity; but at the same time, the new system of transient anti-essentialism is our enemy too, for we also reject the new customized micropolitics of identity management, in which

each human soul is captured and reproduced as an autonomous individual bearing affects and identities.[26] The whatever
rejects the symbolic violence of Facebook just as much as it
rejects the real violence of Jim Crow. The whatever rejects the
farming of "Chinese" just as much as the farming of gold.

In short, there exists today *universality without collectivity*.
The whatever is an attempt to work through this dilemma, not
by eliminating universality, but by showing how collectivity is
the natural outcome of the generic, how the common is only
achieved by those who have nothing in common.

Finally now the unsolved enigma of Chapter 1 receives
some attention. That "dirty regime" called *truth*, consisting of
the intersection of both aesthetic and political incoherence,
returns with full force. The whatever is aesthetically incoherent because it does not coalesce around any given formal
essence or definitional predicate. The whatever finds its
power in incontinence and transformation, not unification or
repetition. Likewise the whatever is politically incoherent
because it tends to erode existing territories and institutional
routines. The whatever is not a coalition or a political party.
No center exists toward which it might gravitate. The whatever
does not make political demands, and has no political platform. A harbinger of the truth regime, the whatever dissolves
into the common, effacing representational aesthetics and
representational politics alike, in favor of direct immanence
in matter.

So the whatever should not be read as simply a new spin
on the same old white liberal hobbyhorse. It is not a call for
all the world's people to appear in our image, for us all to join
in a chorus of "we are the world." No, as George Yúdice wrote,
we are *not* the world. The world does not appear in our image.
By contrast, the whatever is an attempt to avoid the trap of
affect, that is to say, the trap of the "image" of the identity-
bound individual. It is an attempt to avoid the trap of racialized
universalism. The sooner we realize these things, the sooner
we can return to what we are, *whatever* that may be.[27]

Again, to be absolutely clear: the whatever does not elimi-
nate difference. The whatever is neither a synonym for the
universal, nor for the transcendental, the white, the blank, the

empty, or the whole. The whatever begins when the system of predication ends.

To be sure, the whatever is not a panacea. It is not a heroic subject position. The whatever is not a gateway to a utopia. This is not a new kind of Maoism, a call to go forth and disentangle oneself from ideology and privilege, to live among the peasant classes, those who have no qualities except their own authentic history. The whatever is merely a practical suggestion, an ethos. Demilitarize being. Stand down. Cease participating in the system of subjective predication. Stop trying to liberate your desire. Forget 1968. Don't "let it be," *leave* be.[28]

Again the question, was the subaltern able to speak? No, not exactly.

What of today's digital class? It has no choice but to speak, continuously and involuntarily.

And the whatever? The whatever fields no questions and leaves very little to say. Let's try to keep it that way.

Notes

Preface

1   Cognitive mapping is addressed in a number of Jameson's texts including the following: "Class and Allegory in Contemporary Mass Culture: *Dog Day Afternoon* As a Political Film," in *Signatures of the Visible* (New York: Routledge, 1992), 54; "Introduction" and "Totality as Conspiracy," in *The Geopolitical Aesthetic: Cinema and Space in the World System* (London: BFI, 1992); "Cognitive Mapping," in *Marxism and the Interpretation of Culture*, Cary Nelson and Lawrence Grossberg, eds (Urbana, IL: University of Illinois Press, 1988), 347–360; "Marxism and Postmodernism," in *The Cultural Turn* (New York: Verso, 1998), 49; and *Postmodernism, or, The Cultural Logic of Late Capitalism* (Durham: Duke University Press, 1991), 51–54, 409, 416–418.

2   Declension narratives dot Heidegger's later work. It is no secret that Heidegger disliked the sort of life brought on in the twentieth century by capitalism and industrialization: "The decline has already taken place. The consequences of this occurrence are the events of world history in this century. [...] The laboring animal is left to the giddy whirl of its products so that it may tear itself to pieces and annihilate itself in empty nothingness" (Martin Heidegger, *The End of Philosophy*, trans. Joan Stambaugh [New York: Harper and Row, 1973], 86–87). The tone is nevertheless evident, if less cataclysmic, in his early work as well. To take one section in isolation: "Dasein plunges out of itself into itself, into the groundlessness and nullity of inauthentic everydayness," writes Heidegger, after insisting that the concept of "falling" should not evoke any negative connotations! (See Martin Heidegger, *Being and Time*, trans. John Macquarrie and Edward Robinson [New York: Harper and Row,

1962], 223.) If anything, Heidegger's work is special because it entirely synthesizes such an internally obfuscated and withdrawn subject-position directly into a theory of being, rather than either attempting to refine it to perfection (Hegel) or overcome it in pure rejection (Nietzsche).

Introduction: The Computer as a Mode of Mediation

1   Subsequent parenthetical citations refer to Lev Manovich, *The Language of New Media* (Cambridge: The MIT Press, 2001).

2   One common response is that of the schoolmarm, to harp on a strict subject-verb agreement and correct the question as "what *are* new media?" I am perfectly willing to follow Manovich and treat the word media as singular, like the usage of words like politics or aesthetics.

3   Mark B. N. Hansen, *New Philosophy for New Media* (Cambridge: MIT Press, 2004), 35.

4   Ibid., 34.

5   Editors, "Introduction," *October* 100 (Spring 2002): 3–5, pp. 3–4.

6   Brian Holmes, "New Media from the Neolithic to Now," http://brianholmes.wordpress.com/2009/05/22/new-media-from-the-neolithic-to-now/ (accessed June 13, 2009).

7   Lev Manovich, "On Totalitarian Interactivity," http://www.manovich.net/TEXT/totalitarian.html (accessed June 13, 2009).

8   Tiziana Terranova describes such a transformation in her book *Network Culture: Politics for the Information Age* (London: Pluto, 2004) when she discusses the "nonlinear relation between the micro and the macro" evident in informatic media. For Terranova, our contemporary media shift from being a question of difference and position within a dialectical scenario, to being a question of mutation and movement within open systems (28).

9   As Luc Boltanski and Ève Chiapello call it in their 1999 book, recently made available in English, *The New Spirit of Capitalism* (London: Verso, 2005).

10 Cavell's reflections on this are worth reproducing in adequate length: "How do movies reproduce the world magically? Not by literally presenting us with the world, but by permitting us to view it unseen. This is not a wish for power over creation (as Pygmalion's was), but a wish not to need power, not to have to bear its burdens. It is, in this sense, the reverse of the myth of

Faust. And the wish for invisibility is old enough. Gods have profited from it, and Plato tells it in Book II of the *Republic* as the Myth of the Ring of Gyges. In viewing films, the sense of invisibility is an expression of modern privacy or anonymity. It is as though the world's projection explains our forms of unknownness and our inability to know. The explanation is not so much that the world is passing us by, as that we are displaced from our natural habitation within it, placed at a distance from it. The screen overcomes our fixed distance; it makes displacement appear as our natural condition." See Stanley Cavell, *The World Viewed: Reflections On the Ontology of Film* [1971] (Cambridge, MA: Harvard University Press, 1979), 40–41.

11   Cavell, *The World Viewed*, 24.

12   Much more could be said on the question of whether sadism is in fact a suitable opposite for masochism and how and why they might be paired in the first place. For example the necessary narcissism of the masochist, the fact that all trauma must ultimately find both its cause and its solution in the self, also finds an opposite in the "split mind" of the schizophrenic, for whom the fragmentation of the self connects to elements both external and internal, but also enigmatically *within* or orthogonal, to the subject.

13   In Badiou this is both a simple claim about being and a lament of the highest order. The existence of "only" bodies and languages indicates a triumph of a specific political regime, democratic materialism, for which Badiou has zero affection. In a trick of language Badiou reveals the secret: bodies and languages are what *are*, but there are also things that *are not*: truths.

14   He expresses this in many ways in many places, but one convenient spot is Friedrich Kittler, *Optical Media*, trans. Anthony Enns (Cambridge: Polity, 2010), 26.

15   Ibid., 75.

16   Ibid.

17   Friedrich Kittler, "Towards an Ontology of Media," *Theory, Culture & Society* 26, nn. 2–3 (2009): 23–31, pp. 23–24.

18   This position has been endorsed recently in John Guillory, "Genesis of the Media Concept," *Critical Inquiry* 36 (Winter 2010): 321–362. Guillory's thorough investigation, aided largely by the *Oxford English Dictionary* entries on media and related terms, nevertheless, after a brief consideration of Aristotle, discounts the classical and medieval periods entirely. "The

philological record informs us that the substantive noun *medium* was rarely connected with matters of communication before the later nineteenth century" (321). Guillory stresses "a lacuna" of "several centuries," leading to a "long silence in Western thought on the question of medium" (321, 324).

19 Kittler, "Towards an Ontology of Media," 26.

20 Kittler, *Optical Media*, 159.

21 Ibid., 208.

22 Ibid., 227.

23 Note the spectacular finale to Kittler's essay on the ontology of media: "'There will arrive the day when holy Troy has been destroyed', was one of Hector's famous sayings in Homer's 'Iliad'. We cannot predict but gloomingly foresee the night of this fire. Perhaps a rosy new dawn will arise and realize the dream most dear to solid state physicians: computers based on parallel and tiny quantum states instead of on big and serial silicon connections. Then I, or rather my successors, shall withdraw this paper" (Kittler, "Towards an Ontology of Media," 30). I shall respond, respectfully albeit slightly hubristically, that the day has already come. Kittler thinks in terms of seriality. Yet despite the fluttering Turing tape of endless length, one must remember that the computer is a device born of parallelity, not seriality.

24 See Friedrich Kittler, "There Is No Software," *Ctheory*, http://www.ctheory.net/articles.aspx?id=74 (accessed March 15, 2011).

25 Kittler, *Optical Media*, 226.

26 Gilles Deleuze, "What Is a *Dispositif?*" in *Michel Foucault, Philosopher*, trans. Timothy Armstrong (New York: Routledge, 1992), 162.

27 Another thorny shortcoming of the formalist approach is that it is often very difficult to find solid accord between one's formal checklist and the object at hand. I recount a recent lecture as an example. Speaking on "Software Studies" at the University of Amsterdam on August 11, 2008, Warren Sack gave the following list of formal characteristics in defining what computer programs are (or to be more specific, how code differs from other forms of writing): (1) programs deploy the *imperative* (and sometimes the conditional) mode; (2) they are *autonomous*, meaning they can be executed; (3) they are *impersonal*, meaning they eschew pronouns like "I," "me," or "you"; (4) programs are below the level of the naked eye and hence *infinitesimal*; (5) they are *illegible*, as in the inability for humans to read compiled

code; (6) and they are *instantaneous*. Now, I don't disagree with these observations, and in fact believe in the utility of many of them. However as definitional qualities, they all seem rather flimsy. As an exercise I will cite valid counter examples for each so-called characteristic: (1) code comments exist in programs yet are not imperative; (2) computer programs frequently crash putting their pure autonomy in doubt; (3) programs may not use personal pronouns, but variables and variable declaration are at the heart of most programs meaning they are quite fundamentally oriented around the identification and address-ing of objects and entities; (4) consider the example of the computer punch card which is a program that exists at the human level of visibility; (5) open source code formats – HTML even – defy the principle of illegibility; (6) phenomena such as network lag routinely inhibits online games, making their non-instantaneous reality painfully evident. This is not to single out Sack, simply to demonstrate that formalist checklists are often extremely hard to ratify given the complexity of the subject matter.

28   See for example Friedrich Kittler, *Gramophone, Film, Typewriter*, trans. Geoffrey Winthrop-Young and Michael Wutz (Stanford: Stanford University Press, 1999), 34–36.

1   The Unworkable Interface

1   Michel Serres, *Le Parasite* (Paris: Éditions Grasset et Fasquelle, 1980), 107. For the theme of "windows" one should also cite the efforts of the software industry in devising graphical user inter-faces. The myth is branded by Microsoft, but it is promulgated across all personal computer platforms, "progressive" (Linux) or less so (Macintosh), as well as all manner of smaller and more flexible devices. A number of books also address the issue, including Jay David Bolter and Diane Gromala, *Windows and Mirrors: Interaction Design, Digital Art, and the Myth of Transparency* (Cambridge, MA: MIT Press, 2003), and Anne Friedberg, *The Virtual Window: From Alberti to Microsoft* (Cam-bridge, MA: MIT Press, 2006). The best examination of the history and theory of the interface that I am aware of is Branden Hookway's doctoral dissertation, "Interface: A Genealogy of Mediation and Control" (Princeton University, 2011).

2   John Durham Peters puts this quite eloquently in his book *Speaking Into the Air* (Chicago: University of Chicago Press, 1999). For Peters, the question is between telepathy and solipsism, with his proposed third, synthetic option being some less cynical version of Serres: mediation as a process of perpetual, conscious negotiation between self and other.

3   Johan Huizinga, *Homo Ludens: A Study of the Play Element in Culture* (Boston: Beacon Press, 1950).

4   Guy Debord, *Correspondance, vol. 5, Janvier 1973 - décembre 1978* (Paris: Librairie Arthème Fayard, 2005), 466.

5   For an illustration see Ben Kafka's lecture "Anti-Anti-Oedipus: A Freudian Palinode," given in Příbor, Czech Republic on May 6, 2006, the 150th anniversary of Freud's birth.

6   Hesiod, *Theogony*, trans. Richmond Lattimore (Ann Arbor: University of Michigan Press, 1959), 124.

7   François Dagognet, *Faces, Surfaces, Interfaces* (Paris: Librairie Philosophique J. Vrin, 1982), 49.

8   Admittedly McLuhan is sharper than my snapshot will allow. Describing the methodology of Harold Innis, he evokes interface as a type of friction between media, a force of generative irritation rather than a simple device for framing one's point of view: "[Innis] changed his procedure from working with a 'point of view' to that of the generating of insights by the method of 'interface,' as it is named in chemistry. 'Interface' refers to the interaction of substances in a kind of mutual irritation." Marshall McLuhan, "Media and Cultural Change," in *Essential McLuhan* (New York: Basic Books, 1995), 89.

9   I first learned of this delightful satire by attending a lecture by the artist Art Spiegelman at New York University on October 6, 2007.

10   Gérard Genette, *Seuils* (Paris: Éditions du Seuil, 1987), 8.

11   I take some terminological inspiration from Jacques Rancière's amazing little book *Le partage du sensible: esthétique et politique* (Paris: La Fabrique, 2000), published in English as *The Politics of Aesthetics: The Distribution of the Sensible*, trans. Gabriel Rockhill (New York: Continuum, 2004). Any similarity to his ethical-poetic-aesthetic triangle is superficial at best, particularly in that his "ethical" is closely aligned with a Platonic moral philosophy, while mine refers primarily to an ethic as an active, politicized practice. Yet overlap exists, as between both uses of the term "poetic," as well as a rapport between his "aesthetic" and my "truth" to the extent that both terms refer to an

autonomous space in which the aesthetic begins to refer back to itself and embark on its own absolute journey.

2 Software and Ideology

1   Wendy Hui Kyong Chun, "On Software, or the Persistence of Visual Knowledge," *Grey Room* 18 (Winter 2004): 26–51. Portions of the essay reappear in Chun's longer examination of the topic, *Control and Freedom: Power and Paranoia in the Age of Fiber Optics* (Cambridge: MIT Press, 2006). Chun responds to some of the claims I make here in her subsequent essay "On 'Sourcery,' or Code as Fetish," *Configurations* 16 (2008): 299–324, material that also reappears in her book *Programmed Visions: Software and Memory* (Cambridge: MIT Press, 2011).

2   Ibid., 43.

3   Ibid., 27.

4   Ibid., 44.

5   Here the discussion migrates into calls for the creation of a new intellectual field around what is known as "software studies," "software criticism," or "critical internet studies." See in particular the valuable work of Florian Cramer, Matthew Fuller, Geert Lovink, Lev Manovich, Adrian McKenzie, Arjen Mulder, Rita Raley, and Tiziana Terranova.

6   For a founding document on the Java language that discusses this and other language design concepts see James Gosling and Henry McGilton, "The Java Language Environment, A White Paper," May 1996, http://java.sun.com/docs/white/langenv (accessed May 15, 2006).

7   Chun, "On Software, or the Persistence of Visual Knowledge," 37.

8   Michael Scott, *Programming Language Pragmatics* (San Francisco: Morgan Kaufmann Publishers, 2000), 122.

9   N. Katherine Hayles, *My Mother Was a Computer: Digital Subjects and Literary Texts* (Chicago: University of Chicago Press, 2005), 49–50.

10 Espen Aarseth, *Cybertext: Perspectives on Ergodic Literature* (Baltimore: Johns Hopkins University Press, 1997), 40.

11 Ernst Bloch, *Traces* (Stanford: Stanford University Press, 2006), 28.

3 Are Some Things Unrepresentable?

1   Elisabeth Bumiller, "We Have Met the Enemy and He Is Pow-
    erPoint," *The New York Times* (April 26, 2010), 1.
2   Luckily there already exists a number of excellent guides for
    such an endeavor. Particularly invaluable to the themes of the
    present chapter is Susan Buck-Morss' masterly study "Envi-
    sioning Capital: Political Economy on Display," *Critical Inquiry*
    21 (Winter 1995): 434–467.
3   In making such a claim, outlandish on first blush, I do not wish
    to tarnish the powerful and creative interventions made by
    computer artists. The amazing data-visualization art works of
    Lisa Jevbratt or Golan Levin, for example, demonstrate the
    limits of my thesis. The four regimes of signification from
    Chapter 1 will offer some assistance. Jevbratt's work *1:1* for
    example would be labeled "ideological" under my schema, for
    it brandishes a coherent aesthetic (balance in composition,
    color, and texture) in pursuit of a coherent political goal (the
    unveiling of network infrastructure). Yet Jevbratt's counterparts
    in industry are likewise operating within the ideological schema.
    The many maps of the Internet are coherent at the level of the
    aesthetic (tree and only tree) and coherent at the level of the
    political (hierarchy and only hierarchy).
4   Jacques Rancière, "Are Some Things Unrepresentable?," *The
    Future of the Image*, trans. Gregory Elliott (New York: Verso,
    2007), 109–138.
5   These are the titles of two recent books, W.J.T. Mitchell, *What
    Do Pictures Want?: The Lives and Loves of Images* (Chicago: Uni-
    versity of Chicago Press, 2004), and Marie-José Mondzain,
    L'image peut-elle tuer? (Paris: Bayard Centurion, 2010).
6   Rancière, "Are Some Things Unrepresentable?," 111, 110.
7   Ibid., 111.
8   Ibid., 118.
9   Ibid., 121.
10 Ibid., 125, emphasis added.
11 Ibid., 126, emphasis added.
12 See Susan Sontag, *On Photography* (New York: Farrar, Straus
    and Giroux, 1977), Susan Sontag, *Regarding the Pain of Others*
    (New York: Farrar, Straus and Giroux, 2003), and Judith Butler,
    Frames of War: When is Life Grievable? (New York: Verso, 2009),
    63–100.

13   See Georges Didi-Huberman, *Images in Spite of All: Four Photographs from Auschwitz*, trans. Shane Lillis (Chicago: University Of Chicago Press, 2008).

14   Elsewhere Rancière describes three regimes of the sensible, in which Platonism figures as one. See Jacques Rancière, *The Politics of Aesthetics: The Distribution of the Sensible*, trans. Gabriel Rockhill (New York: Continuum, 2004).

15   Rancière remedies this slightly in his more recent book *The Emancipated Spectator*. Although it is not entirely clear that the solution he proposes will be sufficient to address the core problem of representability within the society of control. In typically poststructuralist fashion he suggests that we consider the conditions of possibility for "the opposition between viewing and acting," that we "blur" the binarisms, and "dissociate" cause and effect. See Jacques Rancière, *The Emancipated Spectator*, trans. Gregory Elliott (New York: Verso, 2009), 13, 19, 14.

16   It is not possible here to devote the necessary attention to cinema, nevertheless one might point out in passing that Jean-Luc Godard's *Histoire(s) du cinéma* (1988–1998) has proven particularly inspirational to Rancière, not least because of the important role that the Second World War and the Holocaust play in Godard's argument (if one can call it an argument). Vergil's *hoc opus hic labor est* opens Godard's multipart film, giving the viewer a cryptic indication of its central theme: how does one descend into hell? "The possibility of thinking was extinguished at that moment," Godard has said about Auschwitz. See Jean-Luc Godard and Youssef Ishaghpour, *Cinema: The Archeology of Film and the Memory of a Century*, trans. John Howe (New York: Berg, 2005), 73. For Rancière's writings on Godard's *Histoire(s) du cinéma* see in particular the final chapter titled "A Fable without a Moral: Godard, Cinema, (Hi)stories" in Rancière's *Film Fables*, trans. Emiliano Battista (New York: Berg, 2006), and Chapter 2, "Sentence, Image, History," in his *The Future of the Image*, trans. Gregory Elliott (New York: Verso, 2007).

17   Quoted in Robin Pogrebin and Katie Zezima, "M.I.T. Sues Frank Gehry, Citing Flaws in Center He Designed," *The New York Times* (November 7, 2007).

18   Most disingenuous of all might be the concept of relational aesthetics promulgated by Nicolas Bourriaud, in which relationality itself is aestheticized and exported to the white-cube art

world. See Nicolas Bourriaud, *Relational Aesthetics* (Dijon: Les Presses du réel, 2002).

19   Fredric Jameson, "Class and Allegory in Contemporary Mass Culture: *Dog Day Afternoon* As a Political Film," *Signatures of the Visible* (New York: Routledge, 1992), 54.

20   Fredric Jameson, *Postmodernism, or, The Cultural Logic of Late Capitalism* (Durham: Duke University Press, 1991), 51.

4   Disingenuous Informatics

1   *24*, season 3, episode 4 (Fox, 2003), minute 23.

2   Several technical terms such as "protocol" and "socket" are used by characters in the show in order to give the dialogue an aura of technological sophistication. In *24* a protocol means a directive for action involving information flows and human agents.

3   I thank David Parisi for this word choice, as well as his thoughts throughout. Slavoj Žižek discusses the detached subject position of the *24* torturer in his piece "The depraved heroes of *24* are the Himmlers of Hollywood," *The Guardian*, http://www.guardian.co.uk/comment/story/0,3604,1682760,00.html (accessed January 10, 2006). For Žižek however, this detachment indicates a certain type of coping strategy, not evidence of the pure machinic expedience of torture as a tactic (or rather a *fantasy* tactic).

4   See in particular Lev Manovich, *The Language of New Media* (Cambridge: MIT Press, 2001), 142–143.

5   I discuss this further in *Gaming: Essays on Algorithmic Culture* (Minneapolis: University of Minnesota Press, 2006), 64–65.

6   Anne Friedberg attends these questions with much greater detail than I. See in particular the final chapter of her book *The Virtual Window: From Alberti to Microsoft* (Cambridge: MIT Press, 2006).

Postscript: We Are the Gold Farmers

1   Nancy Fraser charts this historical shift with great facility and insight in her article "Feminism, Capitalism and the Cunning of History," *New Left Review* 56 (March-April 2009): 97–117.

2   Interesting work has been done on the question of race and labor in gaming. See in particular Lisa Nakamura, "Don't Hate the Player, Hate the Game: The Racialization of Labor in World of Warcraft," *Critical Studies in Media Communication* 26, no. 2 (June 2009): 128–144.

3   For two contrasting articulations of this trend see Bruno Latour, "Why Has Critique Run out of Steam? From Matters of Fact to Matters of Concern," *Critical Inquiry* 30, no. 2 (Winter 2004): 225–248, and D. N. Rodowick, "An Elegy for Theory," *October* 122 (Fall 2007): 91–109.

4   Tiqqun, *Introduction to Civil War*, trans. Alexander R. Galloway and Jason E. Smith (Los Angeles: Semiotext(e), 2010), 171.

5   Michael Hardt and Antonio Negri, *Empire* (Cambridge: Harvard University Press, 2000), 137–138, emphasis added.

6   Slavoj Žižek, *In Defense of Lost Causes* (New York: Verso, 2008).

7   Susan Buck-Morss, *Hegel, Haiti, and Universal History* (Pittsburgh: University of Pittsburgh Press, 2009), 138–139, 149, 150.

8   Quentin Meillassoux, *After Finitude: An Essay on the Necessity of Contingency*, trans. Ray Brassier (London: Continuum, 2008), 128.

9   Gayatri Chakravorty Spivak "Can the Subaltern Speak?" in *Marxism and the Interpretation of Culture*, Cary Nelson and Lawrence Grossberg, eds. (Urbana, IL: University of Illinois Press, 1988): 271–313.

10 With the chapter well underway one may now reference the source of this quotation, Cicero's famous lament from the *Catiline Orations* where with much pomp and flourish he decries the abominations besetting the city: *O di immortales, ubinam gentium sumus? Quam rem publicam habemus? In qua urbe vivimus?* ("Oh immortal gods, where in the world are we? What kind of commonwealth do we have? In what sort of city do we live?") Or perhaps for our purposes today a slightly more literal translation of *gentium* is appropriate: "Where are we among all the races?" Are we *barbarians?* Do you think this is *China?!*

11 "Metaphorically patched artifacts [are] technological narrative elements that are brought to fit into the diegesis by the deployment of a metaphor." See Eddo Stern, "A Touch of Medieval: Narrative, Magic and Computer Technology in Massively Multi-player Computer Role-Playing Games," http://www.c-level.cc/~eddo/Stern_TOME.html; reprinted in Frans Mayra (ed.),

Computer Games and Digital Cultures Conference Proceedings (Tampre University Press, 2002).

12   A diegetic machine act is an action performed by the game within the world of the story. For more on this concept see the chapter "Gamic Action, Four Moments" in my *Gaming: Essays on Algorithmic Culture* (Minneapolis: University of Minnesota Press, 2006).

13   See Lisa Nakamura, *Cybertypes: Race, Ethnicity, Identity on the Internet* (New York: Routledge, 2002).

14   Ibid., 101–135.

15   I thank David Parisi for raising the problem of nominalism in this context.

16   See in particular Edward Castronova, *Synthetic Worlds: The Business and Culture of Online Games* (Chicago: University of Chicago Press, 2005). A precursor to *World of Warcraft*, *Everquest* is a massively multiplayer online role-playing game released in 1999 by Sony Online Entertainment.

17   See Barbara Cassin, *Google-moi: La deuxième mission de l'Amérique* (Paris: Albin Michel, 2007), 100, 102.

18   Here I take oblique aim at McKenzie Wark's assumptions in *A Hacker Manifesto* (Cambridge: Harvard University Press, 2004), one of the essential books on politics and information technology.

19   "And she stares indifferently, mocking our imprisonment...," Rey Chow, *Writing Diaspora: Tactics of Intervention in Contemporary Cultural Studies* (Bloomington: Indiana University Press, 1993), 54.

20   Giorgio Agamben, *The Coming Community*, trans. Michael Hardt (Minneapolis: University of Minnesota Press, 1993), 1. Agamben is relying here on the Latin word *quodlibet*; the Italian cognate is *qualunque*, the French *quelconque*. Agamben suggests that the root *libet* indicates that the whatever being has a relationship to desire, yet it carries a slightly softer connotation than that, as *libet* signifies not so much full-fledged desire (a word so loaded with meaning these days) as the fact of being pleased by something or finding something agreeable. Thus one should not see the whatever as a code word for desire in the strongest sense, particularly not in the way that desire was picked up by poststructuralism. *Quodlibet* is literally: "what you please"; or more loosely, "whatever you want."

21   Agamben, *The Coming Community*, 67.

22 To this François Laruelle adds an important amendment. In contrast to both belonging and predication, Laruelle favors the logic of identity in which something is understood strictly through sameness (x is x).

23 See Jason E. Smith, *Optimism of the Will, Pessimism of the Intellect* (forthcoming).

24 Agamben says that the whatever is neither particular nor general, neither individual nor "generic." Yet it is important to point out that Badiou uses the term "generic" too, and when he does he means something very similar to the whatever. So a superficial false-friend incompatibility should not deter us from making a connection between the two terms. See Alain Badiou, *Being and Event*, trans. Oliver Feltham (New York: Continuum, 2005), and also Nina Power's essay "What is Generic Humanity? Badiou and Feuerbach," *Subject Matters* 2, 1 (2005): 35–46, in which she follows an interesting path back to Marx and Feuerbach's *Gattungswesen*, man's "generic nature," or as it is more commonly rendered in English, his "species-being."

25 See in particular Tiqqun, *Theorie du Bloom* (Paris: La Fabrique, 2004). The Tiqqun group also deploys the concept of the whatever in their writing.

26 For a discussion of the whatever in connection with contemporary media technology see the work of Jodi Dean and Dominic Pettman, in particular Chapter 3 on "Whatever Blogging" in Jodi Dean, *Blog Theory: Feedback and Capture in the Circuits of Drive* (Cambridge: Polity, 2010), and Dominic Pettman, *Love and Other Technologies* (New York: Fordham University Press, 2006).

27 Here I diverge – if perhaps not substantively then in a few points of emphasis – from the critique of Agamben and Mark Hansen in the excellent paper by Jennifer González titled "Surface: Slippery Ethics and the Face" given at the "Visual and Cultural Studies: The Next 20 Years" conference at the University of Rochester on October 2, 2009, and published in alternate form as "The Face and the Public: Race, Secrecy, and Digital Art Practice," *Camera Obscura* 70, vol. 24, no. 1 (2009): 37–65. In Agamben the whatever is not a universally same subject, as González's critique of Agamben and Hansen would imply. The whatever is the subject of unassigned difference, not sameness. The whatever is never the same, it never transcends what it is, it always disidentifies itself into the generic. Again, this is a far cry from both the blank, universal

sameness of the transcendental ego on the one hand (the Cartesian, Kantian, Rawlsian variant), and the infinitely customizable granular individuality of the postfordist "dividual" on the other (the cybernetic, behaviorist, game-theoretical, proto-cological variant).

28   For an inspiring example of what this might look like see Eugene Thacker's project "Calamity Gym," forthcoming from Punctum Books.

Index